GREAT COMMISSION

WHAT IS IT?

By

CORNELIUS R. STAM

Founder of the Berean Bible Society
and
Prolific Author of over Thirty Bible Study Books,
Including the Classic Work: Things That Differ

BEREAN BIBLE SOCIETY
N112 W17761 Mequon Rd.
Germantown, WI 53022
(Metro Milwaukee)

IN GRATEFUL APPRECIATION

We gratefully acknowledge God's grace in giving us light from His Holy Word and strength of body and mind to bring this volume to completion while carrying on a busy ministry at *Berean Bible Society*.

We are deeply grateful too for the help we have received from others in the preparation of this book. Some have graciously relieved us of daily responsibilities so as to give us needed time to study and write, and others have helped with typing, proofreading and suggestions. We appreciate particularly the help of Mrs. Virginia Bengston, our secretary for more than twenty years, who did the "lion's share" of the proofreading and *all* the typing of the final manuscript.

Finally our sincere thanks to Mrs. Christine Mulholland for the attractive artwork on the front cover.

PRINTED IN U.S.A.

Fifth Printing 2002

ISBN 1-893874-23-0

EERDMANS PRINTING COMPANY
GRAND RAPIDS, MICHIGAN

CONTENTS

Chapter I

Our Lord's Parting Commission to His Eleven Apostles

Chapter II

The Prevailing Confusion Over This Commission

Chapter III

What This Commission Does and Does Not Say

Chapter IV

The Twelve Apostles and Us

Chapter V

A Serious Side Effect

Chapter VI

Getting Things Straight

Chapter VII

Our Great Commission Still In Force

Chapter VIII

The Necessary Equipment

Chapter IX

It Won't Be Easy

Chapter X

A Closing Appeal

PREFACE

One night recently I jumped out of bed, saying to myself: "Where have I been all these years? How could I be so dense?"

What had dawned on me while half asleep, half awake, was the fact that after all these years we of the so-called "Grace Movement" had not yet produced a comprehensive book on the one subject over which the Church is probably most confused: *Our Great Commission.*

Strange it is that "grace" leaders have published scores, perhaps hundreds, of articles and small booklets on this subject, proving from the Scriptures—and from many different angles—that the so-called "great commission" *cannot possibly* be for our obedience, and that *our* glorious commission is embodied in "the mystery" revealed to Paul. But with all this none of us (to this writer's knowledge) has yet published a good-sized book dealing comprehensively with *our* great commission vs. what is popularly known as "the great commission"—the commission to the eleven.

How sorely we need, how well we could use, such a book to hand to pastors, missionaries, Christian workers and others, providing massive, cumulative evidence *from the Scriptures* as to what our commission is!

That same night I began immediately writing down titles and sub-titles for a possible book on this subject and have been thoroughly taken with it ever since. It is "really something" to have all that evidence before one all at once!

In some 380 issues of the *Searchlight*, covering nearly 35 years, there were many of the Editor's articles on the various phases of this great subject, or directly related to it. Also, in our files there were scores of sermon notes on the subject, along with hundreds of notes written on file cards.

Naturally, it has taken some months to get this all in orderly, readable form, and now having dealt with all this Scriptural evidence and having prayerfully reconsidered much of it, we are gripped with the conviction that even now we have presented only the basic facts.

Thus, though we have sought to make this book as comprehensive as possible, it is by no means presumed to be exhaustive, for the Scriptures bearing on this subject are innumerable. It is our hope, however, that it will provide light and blessing to many who have been disturbed by the lack of agreement as to what our God-given commission is.

Now, as we send this volume forth to our readers, we humbly pray that the Holy Spirit will use our efforts to help many sincere believers to see how wholly unnecessary is the prevailing confusion over *what God would have us do and teach,* and how simple is the solution to this problem when the Word of truth is "rightly divided."

Never has the Church so desperately needed the grace and "spiritual understanding" that will dispel our disagreements over this subject and help us to *"stand fast, in one spirit, with one mind, striving together for the faith of the gospel."* We believe that this grace and spiritual understanding are both blessedly available to those who will sincerely ask God to open their hearts and minds to His truth *regardless of the cost.*

With God's help, then, may each reader reconsider this great subject objectively, asking for an open heart to receive such new light as our heavenly Father may graciously impart.

—Cornelius R. Stam

Chicago, Illinois
December 1, 1974

INTRODUCTION

At a panel discussion on *Dispensationalism* held at Wheaton College, Wheaton, Illinois, in 1947, the author made reference to "the *so-called* great commission."

One of the other panel members challenged this terminology, stating that the commission to the eleven *was "the* great commission," *not* "the *so-called* great commission."

In our response we insisted that this commission *was* the *so-called* "great commission," reminding our hearers that the Word of God does not call it "the great commission"; *men* do.

This obvious and important fact should be borne in mind by those who earnestly desire to "rightly divide the Word of truth" and carry out intelligently God's program *for us today.* Such a recognition would be the first step in the discovery of the root cause of the doctrinal divisions that have separated true believers in Christ and have gripped the Church in deep confusion which it does not seem possible, otherwise, to dispel.

The commission which our Lord gave to the eleven (later twelve) has so long been called "the great commission" that multitudes of sincere believers have a hazy notion that the Bible designates it thus.

The fact is, however, that this designation merely reflects traditional views and, as in our Lord's day, "the traditions of men" all too often "make void the Word of God."

Granted, our Lord's commission to the eleven was indeed a great commission, but it should never be called *"the* great commission," for the ascended Lord later committed a greater, a far greater, message and ministry to the Apostle Paul.

Unless we recognize a change in dispensation with the raising up of Paul, that *other* apostle, the commission to the eleven must stand as an irreconcilable contradiction to the great doctrines of the Pauline epistles—and *vice versa.*

It should be noted throughout this study that the Scriptural term "the eleven" is used only with regard to the period between Judas' defection and death and the appointment of Matthias to take his place. Here, however, a note in the *Scofield Reference Bible* rightly defines the identification as "a collective term, equivalent to 'The Sanhedrin,' 'The Commons,' not necessarily implying that eleven persons were present. See Luke 24:33; I Cor. 15:5; and cf. Matt. 28:16, where 'eleven *disciples*' implies a definite number of persons."

We know, however, that in Acts 1 the number of the apostles is again brought up to twelve. Thus when we refer to the *giving* of the commission, in this volume, we will designate this group as "the eleven," but when we refer to the *carrying out* of the commission in early Acts we will refer to the same company as "the *twelve*."

Finally, it should be noted that throughout this volume we designate Bible-believing Christians as *fundamentalists* rather than *evangelicals*. The rise of the new evangelicalism has caused many sincere believers to refer to themselves as *evangelicals*, but we feel that this term is vague and indefinite, while the term *fundamentalist* historically refers to those who stand for the fundamentals of the Christian faith.

Our Lord's Parting Commission
To His Eleven Apostles

Chapter I

A THOROUGH EXAMINATION

Before going into any consideration of the so-called "great commission," we respectfully request the reader to examine, thoughtfully and prayerfully, all five segments of it, as quoted below from the *King James Version* of the Bible. Yes, you have read all of these passages before, but *read them again.* This time you may see things you've never seen before.

Matthew 28:18-20

"And Jesus came and spake unto them, saying, All power is given unto Me in heaven and in earth.

"Go ye therefore, and teach all nations, baptizing them in the name of the Father, and of the Son, and of the Holy Ghost:

"Teaching them to observe all things whatsoever I have commanded you: and, lo, I am with you alway, even unto the end of the world. Amen."

Mark 16:15-18

"And He said unto them, Go ye into all the world, and preach the gospel to every creature.

"He that believeth and is baptized shall be saved; but he that believeth not shall be damned.

"And these signs shall follow them that believe: In My name shall they cast out devils; they shall speak with new tongues;

"They shall take up serpents; and if they shall drink any deadly thing, it shall not hurt them; they shall lay hands on the sick, and they shall recover."

Luke 24:45-48

"Then opened He their understanding, that they might understand the Scriptures,

"And said unto them, Thus it is written, and thus it behoved Christ to suffer, and to rise from the dead the third day:

"And that repentance and remission of sins should be preached in His name among all nations, beginning at Jerusalem.

"And ye are witnesses of these things."

John 20:21-23

"Then said Jesus to them again, Peace be unto you: as My Father hath sent Me, even so send I you.

"And when He had said this, He breathed on them, and saith unto them, Receive ye the Holy Ghost:

"Whose soever sins ye remit, they are remitted unto them; and whose soever sins ye retain, they are retained."

Acts 1:8,9

"But ye shall receive power, after that the Holy Ghost is come upon you: and ye shall be witnesses unto Me both in Jerusalem, and in all Judaea, and in Samaria, and unto the uttermost part of the earth.

"And when He had spoken these things, while they beheld, He was taken up; and a cloud received Him out of their sight."

Since the subject of our God-given commission is so profoundly important, and since one or more of the passages quoted above are generally considered to be *our* great commission, we suggest that it would not be a waste of time for the reader to turn back and read these five passages again, this time noting carefully just what they say and what they do not say.

Does the passage being read refer to prophecy and the law? What are the terms of salvation? What were to be the evidences of salvation? Does it teach "no difference" between Jew and Gentile? Does it mention salvation by grace, through faith, on the basis of the shed blood of Christ? Does it mention the "one baptism" by which we are baptized into "one body," and made one with Christ? Does it proclaim a heavenly position and prospect for those who believe? Does it mention "the mystery" so often referred to in Paul's epistles?

Such an examination of the record itself may prove to be a real eye-opener entirely apart from our interpretations as presented in this volume.

The Prevailing Confusion
Over This Commission

Chapter II

AGREEMENT AND DISAGREEMENT

There are few, if any, major Bible subjects on which *all* of the denominations and sects of Christendom are agreed. There is one, however, on which *almost* all of them agree.

The vast majority of fundamentalists, neo-evangelicals, modernists and Roman Catholics, along with practically all of the cults, agree that the so-called "great commission," containing our Lord's parting commands to His eleven apostles, contains God's program for the Church today. Or, to be more specific: Most "Christians," nominal or genuine, believe that our Lord, during the forty days between His resurrection and ascension, instructed His apostles concerning *His program for the Church today*, and they all call these instructions "the great commission," or "His parting commands," or "our marching orders."

It is not all as simple as that, however, for especially among fundamentalists, those who study their Bibles most, there has been sharp disagreement as to precisely *which* of our Lord's commands, given between His resurrection and ascension, apply to the Church today: which of them in particular constitute *the* "great commission."

In each one of the four records of our Lord's earthly ministry and in the Book of Acts we have written accounts of *some* of these instructions, but does the term "great commission" properly apply to all of these or only to certain of them? This has by no means been agreed upon.

In the records of the various parts of our Lord's commission there are certain commands or instructions which thinking Bible students have for years found wholly incompatible with the great truths later revealed in the epistles of Paul. And so it came about that most of the great fundamentalist Bible teachers of the past generation concluded that only *some* of our Lord's parting words constitute our "great commission," but they never could agree as to *which* ones applied. This is the legacy they have left to the present generation as far as the so-called "great commission" is concerned. There is little agreement; only confusion and division, where this subject is concerned.

It is sad indeed that at this late date God's people, and even their spiritual leaders, remain in disagreement on so important a subject as to *what God would have us do and teach.* This is written in the year 1974 A.D., and still the Church does not know what its great commission is! This is because the so-called "great commission" is so rarely *examined* and *expounded.* Rather it is mentioned, referred to, and phrases from the record taken out of context as topics for sermons!

Most Christian people have heard their pastors or evangelists speak on Matthew's "*Go*" and "*lo, I*

17

am with you," on Mark's "*all the world*" and "*every creature,*" on Luke's "*ye are witnesses*" and the Acts' "*ye shall receive power after that the Holy Ghost is come upon you.*" But how many have ever heard our Lord's parting words thoroughly and thoughtfully *expounded?* When have their leaders ever conducted Bible studies on the commission which they so stoutly defend as their own?

If pastors and Bible teachers faithfully studied and explained these important commands of our Lord in detail, they would soon find that it is difficult, yes, impossible to reconcile them with the epistles of Paul *unless* we recognize a change in dispensation with the raising up of Paul, God's appointed apostle of grace. Surely the legalism of Matthew's account, the baptism for salvation and the miraculous demonstrations of Mark's, the "Jerusalem first" of Luke and the Acts, and the apostolic forgiveness of sins of John's record are not compatible with the glorious truths later set forth in the Pauline epistles.

What the spiritual leaders of the past generation taught us about the commission to the eleven, must inescapably affect the teachings of our generation. This is the place, then, to back up a generation, as it were, and put the writings of the "fathers" to the test. We do this first as we enlarge upon our writings of thirty years ago in our booklet, *This Is That.* In this booklet we dealt with the deep confusion over the so-called "great commission" among the great—truly great—Bible teachers of that day. As we note this confusion we should not lose sight of the fact

18

that they were giants, spiritually, where many other subjects were concerned.

Dr. H. A. Ironside, long dubbed "The Archbishop of Fundamentalism," held that the Church's commission is found in Matt. 28:18-20 and that to deny this is Bullingerism. In one example of his strong feelings about this he wrote, with reference to the passage in Matt. 28:

"People who have never investigated Bullingerism and its kindred systems will hardly believe me when I say that even the Great Commission upon which the Church has acted for 1900 years, and which is still our authority for worldwide missions, is, according to these teachers, a commission with which we have nothing whatever to do; that it has no reference to the Church at all. . . . Yet such is actually their teaching" (*Wrongly Dividing the Word of Truth,* P. 17).

Apparently, though, our dear brother was so intent on going after the "Bullingerites" that he forgot that many of his colleagues, including Mr. J. N. Darby, the founder of the Plymouth Brethren (with whom Dr. Ironside was for many years associated) emphatically denied that the Matthew commission is ours. We quote here from Darby and several others among Dr. Ironside's colleagues:

Mr. Darby: "The accomplishment of the commission here in Matthew has been interrupted . . . for the present it has, in fact, given place to a heavenly commission, and the Church of God" (*Collected Writings,* P. 327).

19

Dr. James M. Gray: "This is the Kingdom Commission . . . not the Christian Commission" (*Christian Workers' Commentary*, P. 313).

Dr. I. M. Haldeman: "We must call this the Kingdom Commission" (*The Commission*, P. 14).

Dr. Arno C. Gaebelein: "This is the Kingdom Commission" (*Gospel of Matthew*, Vol. 2, P. 323).

Dr. Wm. L. Pettingill: "This we would call the 'Kingdom Commission' . . . It would be a strange thing to find the Church's commission in the Kingdom Gospel" (*Bible Questions Answered*, Pp. 106, 107).

Dr. I. M. Haldeman believed that our commission is to be found in Mark 16:15-18. How he would thunder the words: *" 'He that believeth and is baptized shall be saved.' What God hath joined together let not man put asunder."*

But strangely, Dr. Haldeman did not believe that the miraculous signs of Verses 17,18 are included in God's program for today! You could not join Dr. Haldeman's Church (New York's *First Baptist*) without water baptism, but if you spoke with tongues or sought to work miracles you would be—and some were—excommunicated! Yet these were part of the same commission, yes, the same specific *record* of the commission (Mark 16:15-18). Pastor J. C. O'Hair once wrote to Dr. Haldeman, asking whether *he* was not putting asunder what God had joined together, by thus separating Mark 16:15,16 from Verses 17,18. Pastor O'Hair never received a reply.

20

Dr. Gaebelein held a still different view. Luke, he said, was the Gentile gospel—presumably because it was written to Theophilus (Luke 1:3). However, everything about Luke's gospel is Jewish, not Gentile. Luke's record opens with the baby Jesus in the arms of a Jewish mother and of the aged Simeon, also a Jew (Luke 2:28), and it closes with our Lord in the arms of Joseph of Arimathea, a member of the Jewish Sanhedrin (Luke 23:50-53).

Dr. William L. Pettingill, however, believed that Ironside, Haldeman, Gaebelein and those who stood with them were *all* wrong. Pettingill taught that the Church's commission is to be found in Acts 1:8, basically because in the Book of Acts we have baptism "in the name of the Lord Jesus," which he concluded to be the proper "formula" for our day. However, he never explained, to this writer's knowledge, *why* the "formula" in Acts is different from that in Matthew. Dr. Haldeman was so sharply opposed to Dr. Pettingill's view that we know of one family who, having been baptized in Dr. Pettingill's church in Baltimore, had to be baptized all over again to join the *First Baptist Church* of New York City, where Dr. Haldeman was pastor.

But what about the record in John 20:21-23? Did not our Lord say here: *"Even so send I you"*? Yet this record of the commission was strangely overlooked and barely referred to by the brethren mentioned above and, indeed, by most fundamentalist Bible teachers from their day on. The reason? Those closing words, which the Church of Rome so strongly emphasizes: *"Whose soever sins ye remit, they are*

21

remitted unto them; and whose soever sins ye retain, they are retained" (John 20:21-23).

Some Protestant theologians have sought to explain, really explain *away*, the simple statement made by our Lord here, but their arguments against Rome's position have been as weak as cotton thread, for the simple reason that in this case Rome has always been able to point back to the Scriptures with the reply: "But this is what it *says*." This is always a strong argument and, in this case, a difficult one for Bible-believing Christians to gainsay.[1]

Surely it should be seen from the above that not only has Christendom in general been confused over the so-called "great commission," but our greatest Bible teachers of the past generation have been as thoroughly confused, or at least as hopelessly divided. And if this is so of *that* generation, what shall we say of *this!* The only difference, probably, is that the leaders of our day have been so greatly influenced by the new evangelicalism that they avoid specifics, only *referring* to the commission in a general way as something we should all obey. There is great urgency, but little specific information in their repeated calls to carry out the "great commission" *in this generation.*

If we would find a Scriptural solution to this important problem, then, let us begin by humbly

---

1. Rome's position, however, has been answered, simply and completely, by the application of dispensational truth. See the author's booklets: *The Apostolic Authority of the Twelve* and *Paul, the Masterbuilder.*

acknowledging that the Church has not given a clear, united testimony to the world. Indeed, how *can* we obey our "marching orders" if we are not sure what they are? *"For if the trumpet give an uncertain sound, who shall prepare himself to the battle?"* (I Cor. 14:8).

CHOOSING COMMISSIONS

If we hold, as most Christian believers do, that the epistles of Paul apply to the Church of this dispensation, but *also* believe that our Lord's parting instructions, between His resurrection and ascension, comprise our commission for today, we are indeed in trouble.

Thus it came about that great, truly great, fundamentalist Bible teachers were forced to choose individual records of the so-called "great commission" as binding in this dispensation, in accordance with the amount of difficulty they experienced in harmonizing the various commands with God's Word through Paul. This has naturally contributed much to the deepening confusion among sincere believers today.

As we have seen, Dr. Ironside declared that our commission is to be found in Matt. 28:18-20, but Drs. Gray, Gaebelein, Haldeman and Pettingill, along with Mr. Wm. R. Newell and many others, realized immediately that this would bind believers hand and foot with the law of Moses, for our Lord distinctly commanded the apostles that in going to "all nations" they should *"teach them to observe all things whatsoever I have commanded you,"* and this would in-

23

escapably include obedience to the law of Moses for, not only was our Lord Himself under the law (Gal. 4:4), but He commanded His disciples to "observe and do" whatever the scribes and Pharisees directed them to do *because* these leaders in Israel occupied "*Moses' seat.*"

Similarly, Dr. Haldeman chose Mark 16:15-18 as the Church's marching orders, but other great Bible teachers rightly objected that our Lord here taught baptism "*for the remission of sins*" and miraculous signs as the *evidences* of sins remitted. They correctly concluded that in the light of the Pauline epistles this *could not* be God's program for our day.

It has been said that when some theologians are "persecuted" in one Scripture passage they "flee to another"! And it appears that this is just what Dr. Haldeman did. To prove that miraculous demonstrations are not in God's order for today he appealed to the Pauline epistles, but he did not do this where water baptism was concerned for, *despite the wording of the passage*, he believed that *this* was in order as a testimony to salvation.

A pastor once said to this writer: "Brother Stam, I believe that Mark 16:16 applies to our day, but I don't teach baptism *for the remission of sins!*" We replied: "If you believe that Mark 16:16 is binding today you *should* preach baptism for the remission of sins, for that is what Mark 16:16 commands."

Dr. Gaebelein, as noted above, chose the record in Luke 24:46-48 as our commission, but the phrases "repentance and remission of sins" and "beginning

24

at Jerusalem," rightly convinced other leading teach- ers that this passage, like that in Matthew, is related to the kingdom reign of Christ, which will, of course, be established *at Jerusalem.*

Dr. Pettingill chose the record in Acts 1:8, but this passage too has the apostles beginning at Jerusa- lem.

As to John 20:21-23, almost all fundamentalist Bible teachers have agreed that this is not the com- mission for the Church today, but the Church of Rome surely has Protestants "over the ropes" on this one!

THE FOLLY OF
CHOOSING COMMISSIONS

How foolish and wrong it is for any of us to use "snatch-grab methods," as Pastor O'Hair called them, in ascertaining our Lord's will for us! What right have we to choose some particular segment or segments of our Lord's instructions to the eleven in the forty days between His resurrection and ascen- sion, and to apply only these to ourselves or to the Church today?

Nothing could be clearer than the fact that our Lord "showed Himself alive after His passion by many infallible proofs, being seen of them forty days and speaking of the things pertaining to the king- dom of God" (Acts 1:3). In those forty days, then, one person, our Lord, spoke to eleven men, and gave them instructions as to the program they were to carry out after His ascension. In every single case it is crystal clear that these commands were *not*

25

directed to others, who were to live at some *future* date, but to *the apostles*, who were to commence to carry them out after His departure, when the Holy Spirit had endued them with power.

This is emphasized by the phraseology found in *all five records*: Matt. 28:19, "Go *ye*," Mark 16:15, "Go *ye*," Luke 24:48, "*Ye* are witnesses," John 20:21, "So send I *you*," and Acts 1:8, "*Ye* shall be witnesses." How preposterous, then, to argue, as so many hard-pressed theologians have done, that one or more segments of the commission are to be carried out by *another* generation at *a later time!* By what rule of hermeneutics or logic have we the right to exclude from the interpretation of these commands the very ones to whom our Lord gave them?

Some, agreeing with the above, have concluded that the commission as a whole, then, must be for our obedience, but this too is impossible in the light of the Pauline epistles. Indeed, the Lord has rendered it impossible to obey *any* of the segments of the so-called "great commission," as we shall presently see.

Probably the fundamental reason why so many people conclude that the commission to the eleven is for our obedience is because *they have heard it said so often!* Repeatedly pastors and evangelists and Bible teachers have referred to the Lord's parting instructions as "His parting words to *us*," "*our* marching orders," "*our* commission" and "*the* great commission," as if our Lord never gave any other. But all this is grossly incorrect and unscriptural. These were

26

not our Lord's last words. He spoke again from heaven to and through the Apostle Paul and gave to him a greater, far greater, commission than that which He had given to the eleven.

Before dealing with this greater commission, however, we can, perhaps, best see that the so-called "great commission" is not for our obedience if we carefully examine all the segments of it—*all* of them, in Matthew, Mark, Luke, John and the Acts—and note precisely what this commission *does* and what it *does not* say.

*What This Commission
Does and Does Not Say*

Chapter III

AN IMPORTANT CONSIDERATION

The author, in his youth, heard many messages
on the so-called "great commission," but they were
all devotional or inspirational in character. Though
thrown into contact from his earliest youth with great
men of God from far and near, and rejoicing in the
light they brought on the lately-recovered truth of
our Lord's imminent return, he does not recall one
single *exposition* of the commission as a whole, or
one series of Bible *studies*, in which it was explained
exactly what our Lord did and what He did *not* say
in this commission.

It did not take him long, however, to realize that
the commission to the eleven does *not* harmonize
with *our* God-given message and ministry as later
revealed to Paul and outlined in his epistles.

WHAT THIS COMMISSION SAYS

As we consider all the records of what our Lord
did say in His commission to the eleven, it is impossible to conclude that this commission pertains to the
dispensation under which we now live.

MATTHEW 28:18-20
OUR LORD AS KING

Observe how the first record of this "great commission" begins:

"All power is given unto Me in heaven and in earth" (Matt. 28:18). By "power," of course, our Lord did not refer to physical strength or political influence, but to *authority* committed to Him by His Father. "All *authority* is *given unto Me* in heaven and in earth."[1]

"Go ye therefore. . . ." Does not this opening statement of our Lord's commission to His eleven apostles associate their ministry immediately with His *kingdom* and His *right to reign?* (Cf., Acts 2:29-31; 3:19-21). Thus the passage continues:

"Go ye therefore, and teach all nations[2] . . ." (Ver. 19).

TEACHING THEM
TO OBSERVE ALL THINGS

But what should the nations be taught? What was the apostles' message to them? The next verse gives us at least part of the answer—an important part:

"Teaching them to observe all things whatsoever I have commanded you" (Ver. 20). Are we to obey this specific command of our Lord's commission to the eleven? If we do we will surely bind our hearers

---

1. "Heaven and earth," because the kingdom, or government of heaven was to be established on earth (Matt. 5:3,5; 6:10; cf., Dan. 2:44).

2. The Greek word *ethne,* or nations, is generally rendered *Gentiles* when used in contra-distinction to the *Jews.* However, the *King James* translators correctly rendered it *nations* here, for the apostles were to make disciples of *all* nations, *including* Israel. Indeed, Israel was the first nation the apostles were to bring to Messiah's feet (See Luke 24:47; Acts 1:8; cf., Acts 3:25,26; 13:46).

hand and foot with the law of Moses, its sabbath observance, its sacrifices and all the other ceremonies.

Gal. 4:4 clearly states that our Lord, when on earth, was "made under the law," and the records of His earthly ministry bear witness that this is so. Indeed, as we have seen, the Lord commanded His disciples to obey the scribes and Pharisees *because they occupied Moses' seat* (Matt. 23:1-3).

In this connection it is interesting to note that the disciple who baptized Paul was "*a devout man according to the law*" (Acts 22:12) and that as late as Acts 21:20 those who had been working under the so-called "great commission" said to Paul: "Thou seest, brother, how many thousands of Jews there are which believe; and *they are all zealous of the law.*"

Can we, then, carry out the commission to the eleven without bringing our hearers under Moses' law and contradicting all that Paul, by divine revelation, later taught about the law and about salvation by grace, through faith, entirely *apart from the law?*

But there is more involved here, for in His *Sermon on the Mount* and all through His ministry our Lord had given His disciples many commands besides those contained in the law of Moses. We cite a few:

Matt. 5:42: "Give to him that asketh thee, and from him that would borrow of thee turn not thou away."

Matt. 6:25,26: "Therefore I say unto you, Take no thought for your life, what ye shall eat, or what ye shall drink; nor yet for your body, what ye shall put on. Is not the life more than meat, and the body than raiment?

30

"Behold the fowls of the air: for they sow not, neither do they reap, nor gather into barns; yet your heavenly Father feedeth them. Are ye not much better than they?"

Some have neutralized the force of this latter passage by interpreting the phrase "take no thought" to mean "don't worry" or "don't be anxious," but this wrests the meaning of the next verse, where our Lord calls His disciples' attention to "the fowls of the air," and says: *"They sow not, neither do they reap, nor gather into barns; yet your heavenly Father feedeth them. Are ye not much better than they?"* Thus Verse 25 stands just as it is. As His followers they were to give freely to those in need, nor were they to lay up store for the future since their heavenly Father, who cares even for the birds of the air, would surely care for them.

Little wonder the *Sermon on the Mount* is called "the charter of the kingdom," for during our Lord's kingdom reign His people will spontaneously care for each other rather than for themselves—as indeed they did in the Pentecostal foretaste of His reign.

Our Lord had strong words about the importance of obedience to these commands. As He closed this great sermon He said:

"And every one that heareth these sayings of Mine, and doeth them not, shall be likened unto a foolish man, which built his house upon the sand:

"And the rain descended, and the floods came, and the winds blew, and beat upon that house; and it fell: and great was the fall of it" (Matt. 7:26,27).

When the rich young ruler pressed our Lord as to eternal life and asked, "What lack I yet?" the Lord replied:

"If thou wilt be perfect, go and SELL THAT THOU HAST, AND GIVE TO THE POOR, and thou shalt have treasure in heaven: and come and follow Me" (Matt. 19:21).

This too has been neutralized by the suggestion that the Lord said this to the young ruler because He knew that his riches stood in the way of his salvation. But our Lord had instructed His apostles to do the same!

Matt: 10:8-10: ". . . FREELY YE HAVE RECEIVED, FREELY GIVE.

"Provide neither gold, nor silver, nor brass in your purses.

"Nor scrip [bag] for your journey, neither two coats, neither shoes, nor yet staves: for the workman is worthy of his meat."

Is this the way we should send our missionaries out today?

Indeed, our Lord even gave a similar command to all of His disciples.

Luke 12:33: "SELL THAT YE HAVE, AND GIVE ALMS; provide yourselves bags which wax not old, a treasure in the heavens that faileth not, where no thief approacheth, neither moth corrupteth."

Thus the Lord gave the same instructions to *one man*, to His *twelve apostles*, and to *all of His followers*. As they *prayed* for the establishment of His kingdom (Matt. 6:10), and *preached* that it was "at hand" (Matt. 10:7), they were also to *practice* it, not laying up store for themselves, but rather caring for others and trusting God to provide for *them* (Matt. 10:8-10). This was to be the way of life in the prophesied kingdom.

If we, then, are to work under the commission given to the eleven, teaching men to observe all that

Christ commanded His followers, should we not close out our bank accounts, liquidate all our assets and distribute to the poor? Surely Matt. 28:20 is one important part of the so-called "great commission" which is not obeyed today. Presently we shall see that it *cannot* and *should not* be practiced during "this present evil age."

BAPTISM COMMANDED

Moreover, if we would strictly obey this commission we would have to baptize our "converts" (Ver. 19). But could we then avoid associating this baptism with what John the Baptist said about the subject:

"And I knew Him not; BUT THAT HE SHOULD BE MADE MANIFEST TO ISRAEL, THEREFORE AM I COME BAPTIZING WITH WATER" (John 1:31).

Surely the essential purpose of water baptism had not changed since John, for under the so-called "great commission" the apostles baptized for the remission of sins just as John had done (Mark 1:4; cf., Acts 2:38).

And if we baptized our "converts" with water, would we not be doing what Paul said he had *not* been sent to do?

"FOR CHRIST SENT ME NOT TO BAPTIZE, but to preach the gospel; not with wisdom of words, lest the cross of Christ should be made of none effect" (I Cor. 1:17).

Do we hear the objection that Paul did baptize some? Of course! He also circumcised Timothy, he spoke with tongues, he prophesied and wrought many miracles, but this all belonged to the program under

33

which he was saved and *from which he emerged.* None of these things belonged to his special commission. Thus the fact remains that while the Scriptures state that John the Baptist *was sent* to baptize and the eleven *were sent* to baptize (Mark 16:15,16), it *states* with equal clarity that Paul *was not* sent to baptize. Indeed, if he had been sent to baptize it would surely have been a sin on his part to thank God that he had baptized so few among the Corinthians (I Cor. 1:14-16). All this receives even greater emphasis as we consider what Mark's record of the commission says about baptism.

MARK 16:15-18
WHICH GOSPEL?

Mark's segment of the commission begins with the well-known words: *"Go ye into all the world, and preach the gospel to every creature"* (Mark 16: 15).

The fact that our Lord here sent His apostles forth to preach "the gospel" is to many proof positive that we are to work under this commission.

But is it not illogical to assume that the Lord referred here to "the gospel of the grace of God," which was only later committed to Paul? To this some reply on the basis of Gal. 1:8,9, that the Bible contains only one gospel. But Gal. 1:8,9 says no such thing. How could the Bible contain only one gospel when it so clearly *distinguishes* between "the gospel of the kingdom" (Matt. 4:23), "the gospel of the circumcision" (Gal. 2:7), "the gospel of the *un*circumcision" (Gal. 2:7), "the gospel of the grace

34

of God" (Acts 20:24), etc.? Does a housewife label the jars in her pantry, "peaches," "pears," "corn," "tomatoes," etc., because they all contain the same thing?

In Gal. 1:8,9 Paul simply states that if any preached to *the Gentiles* any other gospel than *he* had preached to them they would be cursed. And those who claim to be working under the so-called "great commission" should consider this solemn passage most thoughtfully and prayerfully, for it is the common disregard of this warning that has brought upon the Church the curse of confusion and division which renders its ministry so ineffective.

Those who hold that the Bible contains only one gospel should also consider that after the twelve had been preaching "the gospel" (Luke 9:6) for some two years, and the Lord, in the shadow of the cross, told them that He must suffer and die and arise again,

". . . THEY UNDERSTOOD NONE OF THESE THINGS: AND THIS SAYING WAS HID FROM THEM, NEITHER KNEW THEY THE THINGS WHICH WERE SPOKEN" (Luke 18:31-34).

In fact we are clearly told in Matt. 16:21,22 that when the Lord *began* to tell His disciples that He must soon suffer and die, He was rebuked for it:

"THEN PETER TOOK HIM, AND BEGAN TO REBUKE HIM, SAYING, BE IT FAR FROM THEE, LORD: THIS SHALL NOT BE UNTO THEE."

How, then, could the apostles have been preaching "the gospel of the grace of God"? They had not been engaged in *"the preaching of the cross,"* for they did not even know that Christ was to die, much less what His death would accomplish. They had been preaching about His *throne*, not His cross, about His *reign*, not His death.

With their message, before His crucifixion as well as after, went the healing of the sick. Luke 9:2 and other passages declare that:

". . . HE SENT THEM TO PREACH THE KINGDOM OF GOD, AND TO HEAL THE SICK."

And in Acts 3:19-21 we find Peter *offering* the return of Christ to Israel and the long-promised "times of refreshing," on condition that they would "repent and be converted." How much those early chapters of the Acts have to say about the healing of the sick! We will deal further with this subject in connection with the "signs" of the commission here in Mark.

BAPTISM *FOR SALVATION*

But more. In connection with "the gospel" which the eleven were to proclaim under our Lord's commission as found in Mark's record, there was water baptism *for salvation*. Could this be stated any more clearly than it is in Mark 16:16:

"HE THAT BELIEVETH AND IS BAPTIZED SHALL BE SAVED; BUT HE THAT BELIEVETH NOT SHALL BE DAMNED."

How shallow is the argument that the latter part of this verse somehow changes the meaning of the former simply because our Lord did *not* say: "He that believeth not and *is not baptized* shall be damned"! If one did not believe would he likely

36

be baptized? And if an *un*believer *were* baptized would that save him? Thus the meaning is clear just as the passage reads. *"He that believeth and is baptized shall be saved; but he that believeth not shall be damned"*—i.e., whether or not he is baptized.

ALTERING THE SCRIPTURES

Bible-believers who hold that we are to work under this commission find it very difficult to accept this verse just as it reads, thus they generally change it to suit *their beliefs.* The most popular alteration of this passage is that made by our Baptist friends. They interpret it to say: *"He that believeth and is saved should THEN be baptized."* But this is not what it *says,* and to alter the Holy Word of God in this way is a most serious offense indeed. It is with such alterations of Scripture that false teaching begins.[3]

The man of God who does this may indeed appear to be *forced* into such a position, since he *knows* from Paul's epistles that salvation is by grace, apart from religion or works and he *thinks* he knows that we are to labor under the so-called "great commission." However, it is always better to wait for further light than to be found tampering with the Word of God.

Remember, the man in the pew has good reason to ask: "If my pastor changes this passage to uphold his own views, what other passages may he change next?" Indeed, he may well conclude that *in this measure* his pastor is already a false teacher. He is

---

3. See the author's booklet, *False Teachers.*

37

certainly not teaching *what the passage says*, and the seriousness of this fact is aggravated when it is considered that the alteration is made in no less important a matter than a divine commission to evangelize the world.

But when a man of God who believes we should be working under this commission, frankly confesses that he does not know how to explain Mark 16:16, and resolves to wait and pray for further light—that man is in the right attitude to receive further light when God imparts it to him.

PETER'S INTERPRETATION

There is another strong argument for leaving Mark 16:16 just as it is. Surely no one would question the fact that Peter was one of those to whom this commission was given, and that he labored under this "great commission" at Pentecost.

Moreover, we read of Peter and his comrades that the Lord had *"opened their understanding, that they might understand the Scriptures"* (Luke 24:45). With eyes thus opened, the apostles further sat under Christ's personal instructions for forty days before His ascension (Acts 1:3). And to cap it all, we read in Acts 2:4 that *"they were all filled with the Holy Ghost."* We shall pursue this further presently, but surely under such conditions Peter *could not* have misinterpreted his commission. And are the terms laid down in Mark 16:16 omitted from his offer of salvation, or does he change or neutralize them in any way? Indeed not! Rather he emphasizes them as he says to his convicted hearers:

38

"REPENT, AND BE BAPTIZED EVERY ONE OF YOU IN THE NAME OF JESUS CHRIST FOR THE REMISSION OF SINS, AND YE SHALL RECEIVE THE GIFT OF THE HOLY GHOST" (Acts 2:38).

Surely Spirit-filled Peter, taught by Christ for forty days, with his understanding opened to comprehend God's revealed plan, would not have demanded water baptism for the remission of sins if he had not been instructed to do so.

MUTILATING THE SCRIPTURES

This affects one more question about Mark 16:16 which should be answered. If Peter was working in obedience to his commission when he told his hearers to "repent and be baptized . . . *for the remission of sins*," where do we find this commanded? Only in the account given by Mark.

We bring this matter up because there are some who teach that the last twelve verses of Mark's account of the Lord's earthly ministry are not to be found in the inspired text. Actually this appears to be a device to eliminate the problem these teachers have experienced with regard to water baptism and the sign gifts.

On what, then, do these brethren base their claim that these words are not in the original? They base it on the fact that the two oldest manuscripts, *Sinaiticus* and *Vaticanus*, do not contain them. We are convinced, however, that one can hardly look into this contention objectively without concluding that the last twelve verses of Mark *were* included in the original manuscripts.

39

First, it must be remembered that we possess none of the *original* manuscripts of the Bible. Second, the manuscripts we do have contain Mark 16: 9-20 in a ratio of 300 to 1. More than 600 manuscripts contain them. Only *Sinaiticus* and *Vaticanus* do not! Third, the Vatican and Sinaitic manuscripts, which do not contain these verses, leave clear indications that they were *omitted*. Fourth, we have translations earlier than our oldest manuscripts which do contain them. Fifth, we have the writings of fathers who lived still earlier, containing quotations from this passage. Sixth, *Sinaiticus and Vaticanus have by now been thoroughly exposed as two of the most corrupt manuscripts in existence.*[4]

The most conclusive evidence, however, that these twelve verses *are* part of the original, is that mentioned above: *the testimony of Peter.* Peter, in Acts 2:38, *did* make water baptism a requirement for salvation, or the remission of sins. If he was not divinely *commanded* to do this we must conclude that he arbitrarily stepped out of the will of his Master. But we know that he was "filled with the Holy Ghost," thus we must conclude that he *did* act in obedience to our Lord's command found in Mark 16:16 and only there, as far as baptism *for the remission of sins* is concerned.

---

4. Here the reader may consult *Which Bible?* and *True or False?* both compiled by Dr. David Otis Fuller, and containing the writings of some of the greatest scholars on the subject. Both contain much evidence of the corruptness of these two manuscripts.

THE SIGN GIFTS

The question of the miraculous signs in Mark's record of the commission still remains. This great subject should be discussed in a separate volume, but since it is so vitally associated with what the apostles were to do and teach, we must deal with it here at some length.

First let us read again, thoughtfully and prayerfully, the exact words of our Lord's instructions to His apostles regarding miraculous signs, as we find them here in Mark 16:17,18:

"And these signs shall follow them that believe; In My name shall they cast out devils; they shall speak with new tongues;

"They shall take up serpents; and if they drink any deadly thing it shall not hurt them; they shall lay hands on the sick and they shall recover."

We often stand amazed at the lengths to which some otherwise objective teachers of the Word will go to explain away those parts of the commission to the eleven with which they have problems! A case in point involves the first statement in the above passage, which has been interpreted by some to mean that "these signs shall follow those who believe *they can perform them,*" or "who believe *deeply enough to perform them.*" The fallacy of this interpretation is exposed by the verse that precedes (Ver. 16), for here believing is clearly associated with salvation: "*He that believeth* and is baptized shall be saved; but *he that believeth not* shall be damned." It is against this background that our Lord continued: "And these signs shall follow *them that believe,*" i.e., those who are saved.

41

Considering the whole passage, then, water baptism was a *requirement* for salvation, and miraculous signs the *evidences* of salvation. If this commission is binding upon us today, then this author is not even saved, for he was not baptized when he believed, nor does he work miracles. This would be true also of many great men of God down through the ages whose lives and labors have borne witness to the genuineness of their conversion to Christ. Indeed, this was what troubled John Bunyan as he considered this record of the commission to the eleven.

But the miraculous demonstrations of our Lord's earthly ministry and of His commission to the eleven had a very particular purpose. *They confirmed His Messiahship.* In Acts 2:22 Peter declared to his hearers:

"Ye men of Israel, hear these words: Jesus of Nazareth, a man APPROVED OF GOD AMONG YOU BY MIRACLES AND WONDERS AND SIGNS, which God did by Him in the midst of you, as ye yourselves also know."

Later, just after Pentecost, Peter stated in connection with the healing of the lame man:

"Be it known unto you all, and to all the people of Israel, that BY THE NAME OF JESUS CHRIST OF NAZARETH, whom ye crucified, whom God raised from the dead, even by Him doth this man stand here before you whole" (4:10).

Thus we read in Heb. 2:3,4 about the "great salvation

". . . which at the first began to be spoken by the Lord, and was confirmed unto us by them that heard Him:

"GOD ALSO BEARING THEM WITNESS, BOTH WITH SIGNS AND WONDERS, AND WITH DIVERS MIRACLES,

42

AND GIFTS OF THE HOLY GHOST, ACCORDING TO HIS OWN WILL."

This "great salvation," which "began to be spoken by the Lord" was, of course, that of Luke 1:67-77, and concerned His reign on earth. And now, under the so-called "great commission" this message was "confirmed . . . by them that heard Him," so that Peter could offer to Israel "the times of refreshing" and the return of Christ upon condition that they would repent and turn to Him (Acts 3:19,20).

These miraculous demonstrations, unlike those of our day, were so evidently supernatural that no one, apparently, questioned their genuineness. Saved and unsaved alike were compelled to acknowledge the mighty miracles of the Pentecostal era (Acts 3:11; 4:14,16, etc.).

LUKE 24:45-48; ACTS 1:8
NEEDED LIGHT AND POWER

There are at least four reasons why we should consider the records of Luke and the Acts together as we determine what the commission to the eleven *says*.

1. Both books were penned by Luke, thus naturally have much in common.

2. Both relate how *before His ascension* our Lord equipped the eleven in a special way for the ministry they were to undertake.

3. Both contain the command to "tarry" or "wait" at Jerusalem for the fulfillment of the promise of the Holy Spirit's coming to endue them with power.

43

4. Both record the command to *begin* their ministry at Jerusalem.

In Luke 24:45 the Lord's commission is introduced with these words:

**"THEN OPENED HE THEIR UNDERSTANDING, THAT
THEY MIGHT UNDERSTAND THE SCRIPTURES."**

No question need be raised as to *which* Scriptures are referred to here, for the preceding verse identifies them as *"the law of Moses, and . . . the prophets, and . . . the Psalms. . . ."* Thus, the Hebrew Scriptures.

Does this mean, then, that these eleven men now understood every detail of every prophetic passage, with no questions left unanswered? Surely not. It means rather that they now had an intelligent understanding of God's revealed *plan and purpose* as presented in the Hebrew Scriptures. This statement in Verse 45 doubtless bears the same sense as if we should say that someone had come to understand the mystery. By such a statement we would not mean that that person now understood *every detail* of this great body of truth, but rather that he now had an intelligent understanding of God's secret, eternal *purpose*, the *plan* which had been "hid from ages and from generations" until revealed by the glorified Lord to and through Paul.

In the context of the Acts record we find a fact quite as arresting, and one that is generally overlooked in connection with the commission to the eleven. In Chapter 1, Verse 3, we learn that during

44

the period between our Lord's resurrection and His ascension He spent *forty days* with them, "*speaking of the things pertaining to the kingdom of God*."

Think of it! A forty-day seminar, conducted by the Master Teacher, the risen Lord Himself! Forty days of teaching, *with the spiritual eyes of His students already supernaturally opened to understand the Scriptures!*

What then shall be said of the many who have charged these apostles, so thoroughly enlightened by the Lord Himself, with being ignorant of God's plan, prejudiced against the Gentiles, etc.? Surely they, not the apostles, are the ones who are ignorant of God's plan.

It has often been charged that the apostles' question of Acts 1:6 was due to ignorance and unbelief. Again, however, it is not the eleven but their critics against whom this charge should be levelled. Consistently the Old Testament Scriptures bear witness to "the sufferings of Christ, and the glory that should *follow*" (I Pet. 1:11). Is it strange, then, that after our Lord's sufferings were over and He had been raised from the dead, the eleven should ask: "*Wilt Thou at this time restore again the kingdom to Israel?*" Of course not. They were correct in now expecting the restoration of the Davidic kingdom, with Christ on the throne. Clearly understanding the prophetic program, they had no question about the restoration of the kingdom to Israel. Their only question was whether this would take place "at this time."

45

Our Lord's reply: "It is not for you to know," however, indicates that there was one great body of truth they did *not* understand, or even know about: *"the mystery."* God's secret purpose concerning this parenthetical interruption of the prophetic program was not to be revealed until Israel had rejected the ascended Christ and God had graciously raised up that *other* apostle, Paul.

Thus the eleven clearly understood the prophetic program, under which they were to labor, but the revelation of God's secret, eternal purpose regarding the Body of Christ, the Church of this present dispensation, was reserved for the Apostle Paul, whom God used to usher in "the dispensation of the mystery" (Rom. 16:25; Eph. 3:2,3; Col. 1:25,26).[5]

All this demonstrates clearly the close connection between the commission to the eleven and God's *prophetic program* as outlined in the Hebrew Scriptures. Moreover, as a clear understanding of the prophetic program was essential to the fulfillment of *their* God-given ministry, so a clear understanding of "the mystery" is essential to the fulfillment of *our* God-given ministry. Hence Paul's fervent prayers that "the eyes of our understanding" might be opened to comprehend this great body of truth (Eph. 1:15-22; 3:14-21; Col. 1:9; 2:1-3).

In both Luke and the Acts we also have our Lord's command to the eleven to wait at Jerusalem until they had been baptized with the Holy Ghost. These

---

5. For a detailed comparison of prophecy and the mystery see the author's book, *Things That Differ.*

46

passages have been erroneously interpreted to mean that the apostles were to *pray* for the Holy Spirit's coming. Many a modern "tarrying" meeting has been patterned after this false notion.

The apostles were not told to *pray* for the Holy Spirit's coming, but to *wait* for *the fulfillment of God's promise* to *send* the Spirit. The precise wording is as follows:

Luke 24:49: "And behold, I send THE PROMISE of My Father upon you: but TARRY YE in the city of Jerusalem, UNTIL YE BE ENDUED WITH POWER FROM ON HIGH."

Acts 1:4,5: "[He] commanded them that they should not depart from Jerusalem, but WAIT FOR THE PROMISE OF THE FATHER which, saith He, ye have heard of Me.

"For John truly baptized with water, but YE SHALL BE BAPTIZED WITH THE HOLY GHOST NOT MANY DAYS HENCE."

And thus it was that *"when the day of Pentecost was fully come,"* the apostles and disciples were *"all filled with the Holy Ghost"* (Acts 2:1,4).

This baptism with the Spirit was, as we have seen from the above Scriptures, for *power,* supernatural power to work mighty miracles in confirmation of Christ's resurrection and to live lives that were completely under the Spirit's control (Acts 2:43-47; 4:32-37).[6]

One more detail—an important one—that is found alike in the records of Luke and the Acts:

---

6. See the author's book, *True Spirituality,* for a discussion of the difference between our Lord's baptism of the disciples into the Holy Spirit at Pentecost, and the Spirit's baptism of believers into Christ today.

They were to begin their ministry at Jerusalem. Luke's record simply says:

"... that repentance and remission of sins should be preached in His name among all nations, BEGINNING AT JERUSALEM" (Luke 24:47).

In the Acts record we have the geographical *order* in which their commission was to be carried out, and again Jerusalem is first:

"... ye shall be witnesses unto Me both in JERUSALEM, and in all JUDAEA, and in SAMARIA, and unto THE UTTER-MOST PART OF THE EARTH" (Acts 1:8).

Well-meaning but confused Bible teachers who insist that the so-called "great commission" is for our obedience, often interpret "Jerusalem" here to be any place *but* Jerusalem. Only recently the author heard a Chicago pastor say: "*Your* Jerusalem is Chicago. You must witness for Christ here first. Then your Judaea is Illinois, your Samaria the USA and your 'uttermost part' the foreign field. You *must* be a missionary at home before you can be used in foreign lands."

We do not deny that it is true that if a man is not a witness for Christ at home, he is certainly not ready for a ministry in a foreign land. *But this is not what our Lord meant in His commission to the eleven.* He clearly had in mind something very different from witnessing first at home.

He knew, and had taught the apostles, that according to all covenant and prophecy the nations were to be blessed *through redeemed Israel*, with Himself reigning as King *in Jerusalem*, the capital

48

city. From here, and under these circumstances, the blessing would flow to the ends of the earth (Gen. 22:17,18; Isa. 2:1-4; 35:10; 60:1-3; 62:1-3; Jer. 23: 5-8).

How, then, could the apostles and their co-workers make disciples of all nations if *the* nation, God's chosen nation, did not first repent and turn to Christ? How could the promised blessing flow from Jerusalem to all nations if Christ was not enthroned at Jerusalem? This is why the apostles were instructed to begin at Jerusalem, and to go from thence to all Judaea, Samaria and the uttermost part of the earth.

How perfectly this explains two little-noticed passages by Peter and by Paul! The first, by Peter, just after Pentecost:

"Ye are the children of the prophets, and of the covenant which God made with our fathers, saying unto Abraham, And in thy seed shall all the kindreds of the earth be blessed.

"UNTO YOU FIRST God, having raised up His Son Jesus, sent Him to bless you, in turning away every one of you from his iniquities" (Acts 3:25,26).

The second, by Paul to the Jews at Pisidian Antioch:

". . . IT WAS NECESSARY THAT THE WORD OF GOD SHOULD FIRST HAVE BEEN SPOKEN TO YOU; but seeing ye put it from you, and judge yourselves unworthy of everlasting life, lo, we turn to the Gentiles" (Acts 13:46).

All this proves with the greatest clarity that God did not usher in the present dispensation of grace at the crucifixion, or the resurrection, or at Pentecost, but later through Paul—after Israel, to whom salvation was first offered, refused it. True, the passage in Acts above refers to a local incident, but what Luke here records about that incident is typical of what was taking place on a national scale.

How much more could be said about the portions of the so-called "great commission" recorded in Luke and the Acts, but the above, we hope, will suffice to prove that this commission is *not* ours, but is rather related to the prophesied reign of Christ on earth.

If the commission to the eleven were for our obedience and we were even now to begin to properly carry it out, we would have to begin at Jerusalem in an effort to win the nation Israel to Christ. And what success might we then expect? Witnesses to Christ are not even *permitted* in Israel, and the few faithful ones who are seeking to "rescue the perishing" there must carry on an underground ministry, and operate as teachers, technicians and what not. If we openly organized a group of a few hundred missionaries to go to Jerusalem to tell the people of Israel about God's grace in Christ, they would be denied entry.

JOHN 20:21-23
THE POWER TO REMIT SINS

"As My Father hath sent Me, even so send I you" (Ver. 21). How can anyone possibly read these words and eliminate them from the commission our Lord gave His eleven apostles in the forty days between His resurrection and ascension? Yet, with all the talk we have heard about "the great commission"

50

and the urgency of fulfilling this commission *"in our generation,"* most Protestant fundamentalists have treated this segment of the commission as though it were non-existent—except in such hymns or devotional sermons as have taken note of the words, *"so send I you."*

Generally speaking, it has only been when faced directly with the words, "Whose soever sins ye remit, they are remitted unto them," that these brethren have even attempted to deal with the passage in greater detail.

It should be carefully observed that when our Lord said. "As My Father hath sent Me, even so send I you,"

". . . He breathed on them, and saith unto them, Receive ye the Holy Ghost" (Ver. 22).

Further, it should be noted that the last phrase of Ver. 22 belongs with Ver. 23, so that together they read:

"Receive ye the Holy Ghost. Whose soever sins ye remit, they are remitted unto them; and whose soever sins ye retain, they are retained" (Vers. 22,23).

In other words, in sending them forth, the Lord breathed on them, imparting the Holy Spirit and divine authority to remit[7] sins.

Bewildered Protestants have found it difficult to accept this part of the "great commission," and in general have vainly tried to explain it away. This, of course, because the claims of the Roman Catholic

---

7. Elsewhere the same Greek word is rendered "forgive."

51

Church to "absolution" are largely based upon this passage.

Some of the denominations also make Rome's claims in modified form in their ritualistic creeds— but with reservations and apologies. Others argue that our Lord here merely gave the apostles authority to *state the terms* of salvation. Others again contend that the apostles were given the ability to *discern and declare* whose sins were forgiven and whose were not. Still others hold that our Lord meant only to impress upon His followers the fact that through *their* conduct some would accept Christ, while others would reject Him. But *all* these arguments wrest the natural, obvious meaning from our Lord's plain words. If He did not mean what He said, why did He not say what He meant?

Rome, of course, contends that our Lord's words in John 20:23 mean exactly what they say, and objects strenuously when Protestants modify, qualify, or in any way alter their obvious meaning.

Since the Church of today is, according to Roman Catholic doctrine, a perpetuation of the organization which Christ instituted when He was on earth—and many Protestants agree—this question takes on enormous theological significance.

In Matt. 18:18 our Lord said to His disciples:

"Verily I say unto you, WHATSOEVER YE SHALL BIND ON EARTH SHALL BE BOUND IN HEAVEN: AND WHATSOEVER YE SHALL LOOSE ON EARTH SHALL BE LOOSED IN HEAVEN."

And to Peter personally He said:

52

"AND I WILL GIVE UNTO THEE THE KEYS OF THE KINGDOM OF HEAVEN: AND WHATSOEVER THOU SHALT BIND ON EARTH SHALL BE BOUND IN HEAVEN: AND WHATSOEVER THOU SHALT LOOSE ON EARTH SHALL BE LOOSED IN HEAVEN" (16:19).

On the basis of these passages, along with that regarding the remission of sins in John 20, the Church of Rome claims that our Lord committed authority in spiritual matters to the Church, represented by the twelve apostles and personified in the Apostle Peter.[8]

And since the Church of today is a perpetuation of that which our Lord founded (according to Rome), spiritual authority resides in the Church, with the apostolic body perpetuated in the College of Bishops, and one of their own number, the Pope, St. Peter's successor, as their chief and the supreme head of the Church on earth.

Protestants may lift their hands in horror at such claims, but next to the Roman Catholic interpretation their own arguments are weak indeed.

Must we then return to Rome, acknowledge her claims and commit our souls to men who can either bless or curse us? No, the solution to this problem is again a dispensational one, a question of "rightly dividing the Word of truth." It lies in the fact that with Israel's rejection of Christ and His kingdom, God interrupted the prophetic program and through Paul, ushered in *a new dispensation*, "the dispensation of the grace of God" (Eph. 3:1-3).

---

8. For a more comprehensive treatment of this subject see the author's booklet, *The Apostolic Authority of the Twelve.*

The majority of Christians still believe, but with many reservations, that the Body of Christ, the Church of today, began under the ministry of Peter and the eleven at Pentecost. But at Pentecost Peter, "filled with the Holy Spirit," said nothing whatever about the Body of Christ. Rather he pointed to Joel's prophecy and said without qualification: "*This is that.*" Thus Protestantism's problem with John 20:23 is the result of a "Roman hangover," the result of following Peter rather than Paul.

If, then, Matt. 16:19; 18:18 and John 20:23 mean what they say, we must acknowledge that divine authority was conferred by our Lord upon the apostles and upon Peter in particular as their head, and that this authority extended even to the remission of sins.

The fact is, that working under their "great commission," the apostles did baptize "*for the remission of sins*" (Acts 2:38).

Was the remission of sins, then, left in the hands of failing human beings? No, not *failing* human beings, for not only did our Lord breathe the Holy Spirit into them *so that they could remit sins* (John 20:22,23), but later, at Pentecost, they were *all* "filled with the Holy Ghost" (Acts 2:4), and with this filling miraculous gifts were bestowed upon them, *including the gift of knowledge.*

This is the answer to those who ask: "Could not some shrewd person have deceived them?" *Did Ananias and Sapphira deceive Peter?* They were carried out dead!

54

Thus the apostles could represent our Lord in His absence, even to the forgiveness of sins, and what they "bound" on earth was "bound" in heaven. Whose soever sins they remitted *were* remitted unto them as they baptized them "for the remission of sins."

Note: we do not teach, as some do, that there is saving power in baptism itself. Not at all. But *water baptism was required for salvation at that time*, thus submission to baptism by water was the natural expression of faith; it was coming to God in the way that He had prescribed. This, in every age, is what has brought salvation.

WHAT THE COMMISSION DOES *NOT* SAY

A consideration of what the commission to the eleven does *not* say is, perhaps, a greater eye-opener than a consideration of what it *does* say.

Unless the author's experience in this matter is entirely unique, it may greatly surprise many of our readers to note that the so-called "great commission":

Does not even contain the word "*grace*," or refer to "*the gospel of the grace of God*."

Does not mention "*the preaching of the cross*."

Does not mention *salvation through the blood of Christ*, much less by *faith* in His shed blood.

Does not mention *Christ's death as the payment for sin*, or His all-sufficient work of redemption as the basis for salvation.

55

Does not offer salvation as the gift of God, *apart from works.*

Does not offer salvation *apart from the law of Moses.*

Does not mention salvation *by faith alone,* apart from the law or works.

Does not associate Christ's death and resurrection with our *justification.*

Does not state that there is *"no difference"* between Jew and Gentile; in fact, it does the opposite by giving Israel priority.

Does not contain one word about *the Body of Christ,* or about our divine baptism into Christ and His Body.

Does not contain one word about *a heavenly position and prospect,* or *"all spiritual blessings in the heavenlies in Christ."*

Under the so-called "great commission," then, we would not be preaching *any* of the above. And when we realize that all this is *the very theme* of Paul's God-given message, and ours, does it not become irresistibly evident that there has been a change in dispensation, a change in program, since our Lord commissioned the eleven?

If the so-called "great commission" is for our obedience and we tell a sinner that he may be saved by grace through faith, apart from works or the law, because Christ died for his sins, are we not working outside, even *contrary to* our commission?

56

It is not until we come to Paul that we learn about "the preaching of the cross" *as good news* (I Cor. 1:18), "the gospel of the grace of God" (Acts 20:24), justification through Christ's finished work, apart from the law and apart from works (Acts 13: 38,39; Rom. 3:21; Rom. 4:5; Eph. 2:8,9; Tit. 3:5; etc.), "the mystery" of the "one body" with its "one baptism," and its heavenly position, blessings and prospect (I Cor. 12:13; Eph. 1:3; 2:4-7,16; 3:1-6; 4:4,5; Col. 3:1-3; etc.).

Yet today pastors and Bible teachers, living more than 1900 years after the commission given to the eleven, and the subsequent raising up of Paul, claim to be working under the so-called "great commission"! Is it any wonder that an ever-deepening confusion has gripped the Church?[9]

---

9. We refer to *theological* confusion, of course, for we are well aware of the artificial union that the new evangelicalism has partially succeeded in bringing about through its false emphasis on love and tolerance.

Chapter IV

UNQUALIFIED OBEDIENCE
TO THE "GREAT COMMISSION"

We have seen that Paul would not have qualified as Judas' successor, for the Lord had said to His apostles:

"Verily I say unto you, that YE WHICH HAVE FOLLOWED ME, in the regeneration when the Son of man shall sit in the throne of His glory, ye also shall sit upon twelve thrones, judging the twelve tribes of Israel" (Matt. 19:28).

Thus it was that Peter, *before Pentecost and the offer of the kingdom,* declared that according to Scripture another would have to be chosen to fill Judas' place—and that this person would have to be one who had "*companied with us all the time that the Lord Jesus went in and out among us, beginning from the baptism of John* [the first day of Christ's earthly ministry], *unto that same day that He was taken up from us* [the last day of His earthly ministry]*" (Acts 1:15-22.)

The choice of Matthias to succeed Judas was made after much earnest prayer (Acts 1:14), in obedience to the Scriptures (Ver. 20), and evidently under the guidance of the Holy Spirit, for we read that "*the lot fell upon Matthias; and he was numbered with the eleven apostles. . . . And they were all filled with the Holy Ghost*" (1:26; 2:4).

This infilling with the Holy Spirit empowered the Pentecostal believers not only to speak with tongues and work miraculous signs, but also to live lives that were entirely under the Spirit's control, so that we find no trace of error or sin in those early chapters of Acts. Indeed, we read in Acts 4:32,33, when their number had grown to more than five thousand men alone, that

". . . the multitude of them that believed were OF ONE HEART AND OF ONE SOUL: NEITHER SAID ANY OF THEM THAT OUGHT OF THE THINGS WHICH HE POSSESSED WAS HIS OWN, BUT THEY HAD ALL THINGS COMMON.

"AND WITH GREAT POWER GAVE THE APOSTLES WITNESS OF THE RESURRECTION OF THE LORD JESUS: AND GREAT GRACE WAS UPON THEM ALL."

This way of life was nothing less than a fulfillment of Ezek. 36:27:

"And I will put My Spirit within you, and CAUSE YOU to walk in My statutes, and ye SHALL keep My judgments, AND DO THEM."

This also confirmed Peter's declaration that the last days had begun.

Thus divinely chosen, equipped and empowered, the twelve apostles immediately began carrying out their commission—all of it.

How futile, then, has been the choosing of commissions by God's people today! How wrong to *select* certain passages from our Lord's parting instructions to bind upon the Church of this dispensation! How wrong to arbitrarily disregard the other passages! Yet this is what is being done by those who believe that *both* the commission to the eleven *and* the epistles of Paul belong to God's program for our day.

The twelve apostles had no such problem. These instructions had been given to *them*. It was *their* "great commission" and they considered it *all* binding, thus they began immediately to obey all of it in detail. Let us now examine all the records of this commission again and see how amply this is confirmed. That their work was *interrupted* by Israel's rejection of Christ and the revelation of the mystery, does not affect the fact that they were faithful to their commission in its entirety.

Here it will be necessary only to deal with such details of the commission as have been, or might be, brought into debate. With the rest there is no problem.

MATTHEW 28:18-20
TEACH, BAPTIZING

". . . teach all nations, baptizing them. . . ."

We have seen that the *King James* translators rendered the Greek *ethne* by the word *Gentiles* when used in contradistinction to Jews, or Israelites. Here, however, all nations, *including Israel*, are in view as noted above, hence the translators correctly rendered the Greek word by our English word *nations*.

The twelve did immediately begin to obey this part of the commission for, as we know from Luke and the Acts, the apostles made their first appeal to Israel, the first nation to be brought under Messiah's sway, and those who truly repented and believed were baptized.

A BAPTISMAL FORMULA?

". . . baptizing them in the name of the Father, and of the Son, and of the Holy Ghost."

As we have seen, some object that Matthew's record of the commission could not have been intended for the apostles because they did not use the "formula" here given, but rather baptized *"in the name of the Lord Jesus"* (Acts 2:38; 8:16). To this we offer a twofold reply:

1. There is no indication that the phrase "in the name of," etc., was meant by our Lord to be a *formula*. They were not instructed to *repeat these words*, but simply to baptize *in the name of*, or *by the authority of*, the triune God, just as a British officer might apprehend a criminal *in the name of the queen*, or an American officer might shout: "Stop, *in the name of the law!"* or our ambassador to France might speak or act *in the name of the government of the United States.* The repetition of words here is not in question, but rather the authority of the representative. Furthermore, when we read that people were baptized "in the name of the Lord Jesus," we must not forget that *"in Him dwelleth all the fulness of the Godhead bodily"* (Col. 2:9).

2. Matthew's record clearly states that this commission was for *their* obedience. *"Go ye,"* is the Lord's simple command, and it is a perversion of Scripture to conclude that He must have meant this order to be carried out by others who will live at a future time.

61

OBEDIENCE TO MOSES' LAW
AND ALL THE LORD'S COMMANDS

"Teaching them to observe all things, whatsoever I have commanded you."

We have seen from Gal. 4:4, Matt. 23:1-3 and 28:20 that our Lord Himself was under the law of Moses and taught His disciples complete subjection to the law. Thus, in obedience to His instructions in Matt. 28:20 the twelve taught their hearers subjection to Moses' law and set the example themselves.

1. In those early chapters they practically lived in the temple. In Acts 2:46 we find them "continuing daily with one accord in the temple." See also Acts 3:1,3,8,11; 5:20,21,25,42. In the last of these verses we read that *"daily in the temple, and in every house, they ceased not to teach and preach Jesus Christ."*

2. We are informed in Acts 22:12 that Ananias, the person who baptized Paul, was *"a devout man according to the law, having a good report of all the Jews which dwelt there"* (Acts 22:12).

3. At the great council at Jerusalem it was agreed *only* that the *Gentile believers* were not to be subjected to the law of Moses. The status of the Jews was not even discussed. It is evident that they had, until that very time, remained under the law, and they evidently assumed that they were so to continue. God had not yet given the twelve any revelation delivering believing Jews from the law (See Acts 15:1,19,21; Gal. 2:3,7,9).

4. In the latter part of Acts (21:20-25), we are specifically informed that whereas it had been "written and concluded" that the Gentiles should not be subjected to the law of Moses, the Jews which believed remained "*zealous of the law.*"

5. Not until the raising up of Paul do we hear any such declaration as: "But NOW the righteousness of God *without the law* is manifested" (Rom. 3:21), or "through this man [Christ] is preached unto you the forgiveness of sins; and by Him all that believe are justified from all things, *from which ye could not be justified by the law of Moses*" (Acts 13:38,39).

As to the *Sermon on the Mount* and the other commands referred to in Chapter 3, they obeyed these too. They *did* liquidate their assets and turn the proceeds over for the common good.

Acts 2:44,45: "And all that believed were together, and had all things common;

"AND SOLD THEIR POSSESSIONS AND GOODS, AND PARTED THEM TO ALL MEN, AS EVERY MAN HAD NEED."

Acts 4:32,34,35: "And the multitude of them that believed were of one heart and of one soul: NEITHER SAID ANY OF THEM THAT OUGHT OF THE THINGS WHICH HE POSSESSED WAS HIS OWN; BUT THEY HAD ALL THINGS COMMON."

"Neither was there any among them that lacked: for AS MANY AS WERE POSSESSORS OF LANDS OR HOUSES SOLD THEM, AND BROUGHT THE PRICES OF THE THINGS THAT WERE SOLD,

"AND LAID THEM DOWN AT THE APOSTLES' FEET: AND DISTRIBUTION WAS MADE UNTO EVERY MAN ACCORDING AS HE HAD NEED."

63

Even the apostles went forth in obedience to Matt. 10:9,10, carrying "neither gold, nor silver, nor brass in their purses," so that Peter could say to the lame man at the temple gate: "Silver and gold have I *NONE*" (Acts 3:6).

This was indeed a foretaste of the wonderful kingdom of Christ, the *"times of refreshing"* referred to in Acts 3:19. What blessed fellowship, with everyone spontaneously living for others rather than for self!

So the apostles immediately began to carry out *all* the details of that segment of their commission recorded in Matt. 28:18-20. They did not, like some today, presume to choose what they should obey and ignore the rest.

It is true that they did not get to all nations with this wonderful program, but this was not due to any failure on their part. As we have seen, it was because Israel, the first nation, stubbornly rejected Messiah, so that God finally set her aside (temporarily) as a nation and, in matchless mercy and love, interrupted the prophetic program, ushering in the present parenthetical dispensation of grace through Paul, who had been our Lord's bitterest enemy on earth but was now the appointed herald of His infinite grace.

MARK 16:15-18
WHICH GOSPEL?

"Preach the gospel."

Many have supposed that this command of our Lord conclusively proves that the commission to the

64

eleven is for our obedience, but this is not so. We have demonstrated by the clearest Scripture that the eleven at that time knew nothing of the gospel of the grace of God. They knew only "the gospel of the kingdom." True, the King had now been crucified and raised from the dead, but this did not change the basic content of their message. Only now, rather than proclaiming the kingdom "at hand," they could actually *offer* the return of Christ to sit on David's throne, along with "the times of refreshing," which every true Israelite longed for (Acts 2:29-31; 3:19-21).

BAPTISM AND THE REMISSION OF SINS

"He that believeth and is baptized shall be saved."

The apostles preached and practiced exactly this. When some of Peter's hearers were convicted of their sins and asked: *"Men and brethren, what shall we do?"* Peter did *not* tell them that Christ had died for their sins and that they could receive salvation as the gift of God's grace, apart from religion or works. Rather he said:

"Repent, and be baptized every one of you in the name of Jesus Christ FOR THE REMISSION OF SINS, and ye shall receive the gift of the Holy Ghost" (Acts 2:38).

Years ago, in a series of debates on dispensationalism, the author asked his opponent: "Suppose, after a Sunday evening service, some of *your* hearers were convicted of their sins and asked you and your co-workers: 'Men and brethren, what shall we do?' Would *you* tell them what Peter told these convicted sinners at Pentecost?" "Why, of course!" he ex-

claimed. *"In those words?"* I persisted. He thought
for a moment and then replied: "Well, I guess not
exactly in those words." The fact is that this pastor
would not at all have said to his hearers what Peter
said to his. Even though a Baptist, he would not
have said: "Repent and be baptized *every one of
you* in the name of Jesus Christ, *for the remission of
sins,*" for he believed that subjection to water baptism should be left to each believer's conscience, and
he did *not* believe that it had anything to do with
salvation. He would rather have said what Paul
said when the convicted Gentile jailor asked: *"What
must I do to be saved?"* Like Paul, he would have
said: *"Believe on the Lord Jesus Christ and thou
shalt be saved . . ."* (Acts 16:31). But Peter, at
Pentecost, preached what he was commanded to
preach under his commission: *"He that believeth
and is baptized shall be saved."*

THE SIGN GIFTS

*"And these signs shall follow them that be-
lieve. . . ."*

Filled with the Holy Spirit, the apostles and disciples also began carrying out this part of their great
commission:

Acts 2:4: "And they . . . began to speak with other tongues,
as the Spirit gave them utterance."

Acts 2:43: "And . . . many wonders and signs were done by
the apostles."

This, of course, did not please the Jewish leaders,
but they could not gainsay the facts. We find the

66

members of the Sanhedrin discussing the situation in Chapter 4:

Acts 4:16: "What shall we do to these men? for that indeed a notable miracle hath been done by them is manifest to all them that dwell in Jerusalem; and we cannot deny it."

And the evidence mounted even higher after that.

Acts 5:16: "There came also a multitude out of the cities round about unto Jerusalem, bringing sick folks, and them which were vexed with unclean spirits: and they were healed every one."

Acts 6:8: "And Stephen, full of faith and power, did great wonders and miracles among the people."

Acts 8:6: "And the people with one accord gave heed unto those things which Philip spake, hearing and seeing the miracles which he did."

It is not germane at this point to discuss the reasons why Paul also wrought miracles, except to explain (1) that God gave him "the signs of an apostle," chiefly as a confirmation to the twelve and the Jewish believers that his ministry was indeed of God, and (2) that these "signs" were wrought during his *early* ministry, until Israel was officially set aside in Acts 28:28.

LUKE 24:45-48; ACTS 1:8
BEGINNING AT JERUSALEM

Luke 24:47: "*. . . beginning at Jerusalem.*" Acts 1:8: "*. . . and ye shall be witnesses unto Me both in Jerusalem, and in all Judaea, and in Samaria, and unto the uttermost part of the earth.*"

This they also did. Indeed, so scrupulous were the twelve in their obedience to these instructions that Jerusalem remained their headquarters even when the disciples were "scattered abroad" by the great persecution that arose when Stephen was stoned to death.

The twelve, Matthias replacing Judas, had begun to carry out their world-wide mission, but had not gotten beyond their own nation. We should always associate Acts 1:8 with Acts 8:1 in our study of the Acts, for Jerusalem, rather than turning to Messiah so that the apostles could go on with their "great commission," had started a "great persecution" against the Church there, with the result that *they were all scattered abroad throughout the regions of Judaea and Samaria, except the apostles"* (Acts 8:1).

The twelve have often been charged with bigotry and unfaithfulness for remaining in Jerusalem at this time. In fact, however, it was rare courage and fidelity to their commission that kept them there while persecution raged and their very lives were in danger. They remained at Jerusalem for the same reason that the rest fled: because Jerusalem was *not* turning to Christ. The first part of their commission had not yet been completed, therefore they were duty-bound to remain there.

Certainly the twelve did not remain at Jerusalem because they were prejudiced against the salvation of the Gentiles. There is too much Scriptural evidence against this. Rather, they remained there because they had a clear understanding of the prophetic program and of their Lord's commission. They knew

68

that according to covenant and prophecy the Gentiles were to be saved and blessed *through redeemed Israel* (Gen. 22:17,18; Isa. 60:1-3; Zech. 8:13). Our Lord had indicated no change in this program, and He Himself had worked in perfect harmony with it. Before His death He had insisted that Israel was *first* in God's revealed program, commanding His disciples not to go to the Gentiles or the Samaritans, but to *"go rather to the lost sheep of the house of Israel"* (Matt. 10:6), and saying to a Gentile woman who came for help: *"Let the children first be filled"* (Mark 7:27). And now, in His "great commission" to the eleven, He specifically stated that they should *begin at Jerusalem,* as we have seen above.

It is amazing that some should charge the twelve apostles and the Jewish believers with prejudice against the Gentiles because they did not immediately go "to the uttermost part of the earth," when they were explicitly *told* by the Lord to make disciples of all nations *beginning at Jerusalem* and when there is so much evidence that they longed for the salvation of the Gentiles and rejoiced when Gentiles turned to Christ (See Acts 3:25; 10:9,15; 11:18,23,24; 15:3; 21:19,20).

Which took the greater courage, to flee from Jerusalem now or to remain there in the raging persecution, in daily peril of death? Would not unfaithful men have fled at such a time? We are not blaming the multitude of the disciples for fleeing for their lives, but are rather giving the twelve due credit for faithfully carrying out the orders specifically given them.

69

JOHN 20:21-23
REMITTING SINS

"Whose soever sins ye remit, they are remitted unto them."

The apostles were surely laboring under this part of their commission when they baptized their convicted hearers *"for the remission of sins"* (Acts 2: 38,41).

At the series of debates on dispensationalism referred to earlier, our opponent asked: "Do you mean to tell us that Peter, at Pentecost, did *not* proclaim the gospel of the grace of God?" I responded that this was exactly what I believed. This amazed him, so I asked him to define the gospel of the grace of God. To this he replied correctly: "We'd have no disagreement on that. I believe that the gospel of the grace of God is that we are sinners, condemned to judgment, but that because Christ died for our sins we may be saved by grace through faith in Him, plus nothing." I then asked him whether he could find this in Peter's Pentecostal address. "Yes," he said. However, we had agreed that in this debate questions would be answered by the Word of God alone, so he stood looking at Acts 2 for some time, until finally he continued: "Well, it does say here in Verse 21 that 'Whosoever shall call upon the name of the Lord shall be saved,' but I know what you'll say about that." "What will I say?" I asked. To this he replied: "Well, I guess you'll say that when they did call Peter said, 'Repent and be baptized for the remission of sins.'" "Yes," I replied, "that is exactly what the record says."

70

Those who, like this pastor, have supposed that Peter at Pentecost proclaimed "the gospel of the grace of God," should ask themselves why he did not tell them that Christ had died for their sins, so that they might be saved by grace, through faith alone; why, instead, he demanded repentance and baptism for the remission of sins.

Doubtless this is what is back of Paul's statement in I Cor. 1:17: "For CHRIST SENT ME NOT TO BAPTIZE, but to preach the gospel:[1] not with wisdom of words LEST THE CROSS OF CHRIST SHOULD BE MADE OF NONE EFFECT." This, *the cross*, was the heart of Paul's God-given message. This is what *he* preached "for the remission of sins," and this is why his gospel is also called, "*the preaching of the cross*" (I Cor. 1:18).

Mark 1:4 states plainly that John the Baptist preached "THE BAPTISM OF REPENTANCE FOR THE REMISSION OF SINS." This part of God's program was not changed by the commission to the eleven. The great change came later, with the raising up of Paul, the chief of sinners saved by grace. *He* declared that Christ had *not* sent him to baptize (as John and the eleven had been sent) but to preach the gospel—"the gospel of the grace of God."

THE IMPOSSIBILITY OF CARRYING OUT
THIS COMMISSION TODAY

From the foregoing it should now be clear that the commission to the eleven *cannot* be carried out

---

1. The gospel committed to *him,* of course (Acts 20:24).

71

today—and that no one *is* carrying it out. God has rendered this impossible.

Let us now review briefly all the individual details of the commission to confirm this statement.

MATTHEW'S ACCOUNT
MATTHEW 28:18-20

"All power. . . ."

This has nothing to do with the dispensation of grace or the Body of Christ. As we have seen, it refers to our Lord's *authority* to reign as King of the "kingdom of heaven" to be established on earth (Matt. 5:3,5; 6:10).

"Go ye therefore. . . ."

The eleven were sent forth *because* all authority was His, and were to proclaim His royal rights. If this were our commission our great message would be our Lord's throne and His authority, rather than His cross and His grace. *Could* we preach this today in the light of the subsequent setting aside of Israel and the infinite grace that flows from Calvary? (See Rom. 11:25,32; I Cor. 15:1-3; II Cor. 5:21; Eph. 2:13-16; etc.).

"Teach all nations. . . ."

This would bring in the fulfillment of Isa. 2:1-3, not the forming of the Body of Christ.

"Teaching them to observe all things whatsoever I have commanded you. . . ."

If this were our commission it would, as we have shown, put us and our hearers under the law of Moses (Gal. 4:4; Matt. 23:1-3). How *could* we teach this in the light of perhaps a hundred clear passages from Paul's epistles, including the following:

Rom. 3:21: "But now the righteousness of God WITHOUT THE LAW IS manifested. . . ."

Gal. 3:13: "CHRIST HATH REDEEMED US FROM THE CURSE OF THE LAW, being made a curse for us. . . ."

Rom. 6:14: "For sin shall not have dominion over you: for YE ARE NOT UNDER THE LAW, BUT UNDER GRACE."

Gal. 2:21: "I DO NOT FRUSTRATE THE GRACE OF GOD: FOR IF RIGHTEOUSNESS COME BY THE LAW, THEN CHRIST IS DEAD [HAS DIED] IN VAIN."

But this part of the so-called "great commission" would also subject us to the precepts of the *Sermon on the Mount* and *all* that our Lord commanded while on earth. We have seen how He said to all of His disciples: *"Sell that ye have and give alms"* (Luke 12:33), and bade them forbear making provisions for the future (Vers. 22-31).

This command is clear enough. *They* understood and obeyed it. But we do not and *cannot* obey it today. Indeed, if we did liquidate our assets and distribute the proceeds to the poor; if we did forbear making provisions for the future, we would be *dis*obeying the command of our *ascended* Lord regarding this very matter, for in I Tim. 5:8 the inspired apostle declares:

"BUT IF ANY PROVIDE NOT FOR HIS OWN, AND SPECIALLY FOR THOSE OF HIS OWN HOUSE, HE HATH DENIED THE FAITH, AND IS WORSE THAN AN INFIDEL [UNBELIEVER]."

True, in the same letter the apostle bids us to be rich in good works and to be generous contributors to the cause of Christ, but the fact remains that whereas our Lord *on earth* bade His followers *not* to provide for future needs, He *now* bids *us* to do so if we would be true to "the faith," i.e., the "one faith" proclaimed by Paul for this present dispensation (Eph. 4:5).

If it were not so distressing it would be humorous to observe what many of our "great commission" friends do with Luke 12:31-33.

A favorite, frequently quoted, is Verse 31:

"But rather seek ye the kingdom of God, and all these things shall be added unto you."

The trouble is, however, that they misinterpret this to mean, "Seek ye the *things* of God." They just cannot imagine *seeking* the *kingdom*. Thus when they reach Verse 32 their interpretation becomes more ambiguous. The verse itself is clear enough.

"Fear not, little flock; for it is your Father's good pleasure TO GIVE YOU THE KINGDOM."

Having already changed the simple meaning of Verse 31, however, they now interpret "the kingdom," in Verse 32, to mean "spiritual victory" or something of the sort.

But Verse 33: *"Sell that ye have and give alms,"* *really* presents problems! Moreover the language is so simple that it *cannot* be altered to mean something else. Result: they take two aspirin tablets, as it were, and try to forget it! How significant it is that the very ones who make so much of Luke 12:31,32, never seem to even quote Verse 33, and *certainly never practice it!*

Actually, the meaning of the whole passage is simple as ABC when we rightly divide the Word of truth. Our Lord is simply telling His disciples that it is His Father's good pleasure to *give them* the kingdom, to place them in authority, and that if they will "seek" it even now "all these things" (needed food and clothing) will be amply provided for them. Thus He goes on: *"Sell that ye have and give alms."* It is as simple as that.

In any case, they did *not*, like many today, take lightly our Lord's words in Matt. 7:24-27, but, filled with the Holy Spirit, immediately set out to obey their commission to the letter. Unless we are prepared to do the same we had better acknowledge that there has since been a change in dispensation.

"Baptizing them. . . ."

This would take us back under a dispensation when, as we have seen, water baptism was required *for the remission of sins.* This would indeed make the cross of Christ "of none effect." Nowhere in Paul's epistles is there one command or even a suggestion that we should be baptized with water. It is true that some *read water into* Rom. 6:3; Gal. 3:27 and Col. 2:12, but these verses do not mention water or refer to water baptism, and those who read water baptism into them promote "the traditions of the fathers," "make void the Word of God," and unwittingly rob sincere believers of their most precious possessions (Col. 2:8-12).

As we have seen, Paul declares in I Cor. 1:17 that water baptism was not part of his special commission. True, *during his early ministry* he baptized some; he also circumcised Timothy, spoke with tongues, prophesied and wrought miracles. Should we practice all these? No, for, as we have seen, this was the dispensation under which he was saved and *from which he emerged* as the glorified Lord gradually revealed to him "the dispensation of the grace of God" and the truths associated with "the mystery" (Acts 26:16; II Cor. 12:1,7). The very *theme* of Paul's great message is that all believers *have been* baptized into "one body," the Body of Christ, and thus into Christ Himself, by *"one* baptism," that which is performed "by *the operation of God"* (Rom. 6:3; I Cor. 12:13; Gal. 3:26,27; Col. 2:10,12; Eph. 4:5).

"And, lo, I am with you alway, even unto the end of the world.[2] Amen."

Many, not understanding the parenthetical character of the "mystery" proclaimed by Paul, have concluded on the basis of this promise that our commission is a perpetuation of that given by our Lord to the eleven apostles. On the contrary, however, it is another evidence of the fact that the interruption of the prophetic program by "the dispensation of the grace of God" was then still a secret concerning

---

2. Or, "age."

which our Lord could reveal nothing. How often Paul insists that the revelation committed to him had been *"kept secret since the world began"* (Rom. 16:25), a *"mystery . . . in other ages not made known. . . . hid in God"* (Eph. 3:9), *"hid from ages and from generations, but NOW . . . made manifest to His saints"* (Col. 1:26). Thus our Lord, in His statement, looked beyond this entire parenthetical dispensation to the end of the "age" that pertained *to them and their labors.*

MARK'S ACCOUNT
MARK 16:15-18

"Preach the gospel. . . ."

To ascertain the content of this gospel we may not anticipate revelation and find our answer in the Acts or Paul's epistles. These were not yet written. The term *"the* gospel" denotes *prior reference,* therefore we must consider *the preceding context* and ask ourselves what "gospel" they *had been* preaching. When we do this the answer is simple. They had been preaching *"the gospel of the kingdom"* (Matt. 4:23; 9:35; 24:14; Mark 1:14,15; Luke 4:43; 8:1; 9:2,60), and our Lord was now sending them forth to preach this same gospel, for the King who had been crucified was alive again; raised from the dead to sit on the throne of David. And this is in fact what Peter preached under this commission (Acts 2:29,30; 3:19-21). The gospel of the grace of God was not revealed until years later through Paul (Acts 20:24).

We cannot preach the "gospel" of Mark 16 today, for the risen King was again rejected by His own nation and is now a royal Exile.

"He that believeth and is baptized shall be saved. . . ."

How could we possibly preach this without contradicting Rom. 3:24; 4:5; I Cor. 1:17 (Cf. 4:16; 11:1), Eph. 2:8-10; 4:5; Tit. 3:5 and many other passages from Paul's epistles?

"And these signs shall follow them that believe":

The fulfillment of this part of the so-called "great commission" has indeed been rendered *impossible*. We have already accounted for the many alleged miracles performed by the Roman Catholic Church, the Christian Scientists, the Unity Movement and other cults and sects, plus our Pentecostalist brethren, but the promise to the eleven was clear and emphatic: "These signs SHALL follow THEM THAT BELIEVE," and today believers in general are *not* performing any of these great miracles. Where they are seemingly, or allegedly, being performed they are for the most part held suspect by many, while even the rankest unbelievers acknowledged the mighty miracles wrought under the commission given to the eleven.[3]

It should be noted here that since these miracles were *signs* of our Lord's Messiahship and evidences that His kingdom was "at hand" (Isa. 35:5,6), all

---

3. Here see the author's booklets, *This Is That* and *Are the Pentecostal Signs Being Restored?*

those who were healed would have lived right on indefinitely had Israel accepted the King and His kingdom. But the King was rejected, so they all died again and to this day the death rate remains "one apiece." This explains the words "until now" in Rom. 8:22.

This is the place to discuss more fully the passing of the sign gifts.

THE SIGN GIFTS WITHDRAWN

Obviously, if we are to work under the commission to the eleven we should, like them, be working miracles—miracles whose genuineness is self-evident. However, there is much reason to question—and many do question—the genuineness of the alleged "Pentecostal gifts" claimed by many today. The "gift" of tongues, increasingly widespread, and the alleged power to exorcise demons, have been questioned by many students of the Word. As to the supposed gift of healing claimed by our Pentecostalist friends, the fact must not be overlooked that the Roman Church, the Christian Scientists and the Unity Movement can present "evidences" fully as convincing. Are their powers, then, also God-given?

A long list could be compiled, containing the names of popular preachers and evangelists who, through the years, have told their audiences that God would have all of us to be sound in body and that continued illness evidences a lack of faith—*and then themselves succumbed to death.* The list would read like that in Genesis 5, interspersing the records

79

of them all with the words: *"and he died. . . . and he died. . . . and he died."*

The fact is that the miraculous signs promised in Mark 16:17,18 and practiced in early Acts, were "done away" with the ushering in of "the dispensation of the grace of God." This is confirmed by many facts and statements from the record of Scripture.

In I Cor. 13:8 we have Paul's Spirit-inspired declaration: ". . . *whether there be prophecies, they shall fail; whether there be tongues, they shall cease; whether there be knowledge, it shall vanish away.*"

Obviously the apostle did not mean that divine prophecies would fail *to come to pass*, or that men would stop *talking* or *knowing*. He referred, of course, to the supernatural *gifts* of prophecy, tongues and knowledge (Peter demonstrated the gift of knowledge in the case of Ananias and Sapphira). These gifts were to be "done away" and would "cease."

But the cessation of the supernatural sign gifts is further confirmed by incidents in Paul's own life and ministry. When he was imprisoned, in Acts 16, an earthquake shook the foundations of the prison, opening every prisoner's door—*and* loosing every man's *bands* (Ver. 26). His later epistles, however, reveal the apostle abandoned to imprisonment without any miracle of deliverance (Eph. 6:18-20; Col. 4:18; II Tim. 2:9).

Similarly the great apostle, by whose hands God had wrought "special miracles" (Acts 19:11), himself suffered bodily infirmities (Gal. 4:13) and a particular "thorn in the flesh" that caused him much suffering and pain. He prayed earnestly that he might be delivered from this painful affliction, but *God did not grant his request,* promising him instead His own all-sufficient grace to help him bear his lot, and assuring him: *"My strength is made perfect in weakness"* (II Cor. 12:8,9). The apostle accepted this in true faith and later declared:

". . . most gladly therefore will I rather glory in mine infirmities, THAT THE POWER OF CHRIST MAY REST UPON ME.

"Therefore I take pleasure in infirmities, in reproaches, in necessities, in distresses for Christ's sake; for WHEN I AM WEAK, THEN AM I STRONG" (Vers. 9,10).

The passing of the healing gifts is still further confirmed by incidents in Paul's association with his friends. He writes to the Philippians about Epaphroditus who had been "sick nigh unto death." Unable to relate that he, Paul, had been empowered to heal him, the apostle says: *"God had mercy on him; and . . . on me also, lest I should have sorrow upon sorrow"* (Phil. 2:27). Similarly, in II Tim. 4:20 he says: *"Trophimus have I left at Miletum sick,"* and for Timothy's recurring illness he prescribes *"a little wine"* (I Tim. 5:23). All this indicates that the apostle's healing powers had been withdrawn—and it all sounds, *not* like the Pentecostal era, but rather like the day in which we live.

In addition to Gal. 4:13 and II Cor. 12:8,9, many other passages give clear evidence that the apostle himself was anything but a well man, physically, and that he realized that this was now to be the common

81

lot, not only of mankind in general, but also of God's saints. Let us consider some of these.

Rom. 8:22,23: "For we know that THE WHOLE CREATION GROANETH AND TRAVAILETH IN PAIN together until now.

"And not only they, but OURSELVES ALSO, which have the firstfruits of the Spirit, even WE OURSELVES GROAN WITHIN OURSELVES, WAITING FOR THE ADOPTION, TO WIT, THE REDEMPTION OF OUR BODY."

II Cor. 5:2,4: For IN THIS [TABERNACLE] WE GROAN, earnestly desiring to be clothed upon with our house which is from heaven."

"For WE THAT ARE IN THIS TABERNACLE DO GROAN, being burdened: not for that we would be unclothed, but clothed upon, that mortality might be swallowed up of life."

II Cor. 4.16: "For the which cause we faint not; but THOUGH OUR OUTWARD MAN PERISH, yet the inward man is renewed day by day."

II Cor. 12:7: "And lest I should be exalted above measure through the abundance of the revelations, THERE WAS GIVEN TO ME A THORN IN THE FLESH, A MESSENGER OF SATAN TO BUFFET ME, LEST I SHOULD BE EXALTED ABOVE MEASURE."

If Paul were with us today, he would be sternly censured by those who teach that it is lack of faith and a sin not to claim physical healing. They do not know the joy of the all-sufficient grace that sustained Paul *in* sickness and adversity, nor have they seen how God's strength is "*made perfect in weakness.*" This is why they cannot, with him, rejoice in their infirmities, finding God's strength in their weakness.

What a volume of evidence all the above provides in confirmation of the fact that the healing

82

miracles of the so-called "great commission" have passed away, to be replaced by something better.

Better? Indeed, for is not deliverance *in* sickness a far greater victory than deliverance *from* sickness? Is not joy *in* prison (Eph. 1:3; Phil. 1:12-14; 3:1; 4:4-7) a far greater blessing than release *from* prison? Is not God's power enhanced in far greater measure through our weakness than it ever could be through our "strength"? Is there a greater joy than *experiencing* His all-sufficient grace?

THE COMMISSION IN LUKE AND THE ACTS
LUKE 24:46-48 and ACTS 1:8

"Beginning at Jerusalem." "Jerusalem . . . all Judaea . . . Samaria . . . the uttermost part of the earth."

We have seen that today it would be as impossible, as it would be foolish, to attempt to carry out the so-called "great commission" by beginning again at Jerusalem which, even yet, has not been brought to Messiah's feet.

Should a group of missionaries wish to preach the gospel there they would either have to enter as something other than Christian missionaries and work underground, or they would be deported forthwith. Great credit is due those doctors, nurses, etc., who have entered as such and have been able to show individual Israelites that God loves them and that Christ died to save them. But this is something very different from launching a campaign to preach "the gospel of the kingdom" in the city of Jerusalem as the apostles did.

"And ye are witnesses of these things."

What things? Very evidently the apostles were witnesses of the death and resurrection of the rejected King. The contexts in both Luke and the Acts bear this out. Remember, neither the death nor the resurrection of Christ were then being preached as they were later proclaimed under the revelation committed to Paul. Under their commission the twelve did not preach the death and resurrection of Christ as good news. They rather *accused* their hearers of Christ's death and *warned* them that He was alive again (See Acts 2:23,30,31,36; 3:13-15; 4:10). Their good news was that Israel could now repent and that Christ would then return, and with Him the long-promised "times of refreshing" (Acts 3:19-21,25,26).

"Tarry ye in the city of Jerusalem, until ye be endued with power from on high."

The twelve were to be "endued with power from on high" at the fulfillment of "the promise of the Father," i.e., the coming of the Holy Spirit. But Pentecost is now long gone, and the phrase, "they were ALL filled with the Holy Ghost," stands in sharp contrast to the lack of the Spirit's infilling in the Church today. Also, the miraculous signs, the outward manifestations of the Spirit's filling, were withdrawn with the passing of that dispensation.

And shall we now wait *again* for the fulfillment of the promise, "Ye shall receive power after that the Holy Ghost is come upon you"? This is what some are doing, even though this promise was fulfilled in due time, "when the day of Pentecost was fully come." Nowhere in Paul's epistles—or anywhere else—are we instructed to wait for *another* fulfillment of this promise, much less are we told to *pray* for the coming of the Holy Spirit. Indeed, with the passing of Pentecost the recovery of *Pentecostal* power has been rendered impossible. How unscriptural and unwarranted, then, are the "tarrying meetings" of modern Pentecostalism!

It should be carefully noted here that while *all* the believers at Pentecost were *filled* with the Holy Spirit (Acts 2:4), it is never indicated that the whole Church, or all the members of any *local* church of Paul's day were filled with the Holy Spirit. The Galatian believers were certainly not "all filled with the Holy Spirit"; they "bit and devoured one another" (Gal. 5:15). The Philippian believers were certainly not "all filled with the Holy Spirit"; there was dissension there between two of the women— and those who sided with each (Phil. 4:1-3). The Colossian saints were certainly not "all filled with the Holy Spirit"; they had entertained notions of gnosticism, which Paul had to correct (Col. 2:8,18-23). The Thessalonian believers were certainly not "all filled with the Holy Spirit"; they had failed to heed Paul's word regarding the coming of Christ for the members of His Body and were in fear about their departed loved ones (I Thes. 4:13; II Thes. 2:5). There were other moral and spiritual deficiencies among all the members of all of the churches founded by Paul, as there are among all the members of the Church today. See Paul's personal testimony as to

85

this in Rom. 7:18-25; Phil. 3:12-14. Rather than "all" of us being filled with the Holy Spirit, *completely* under His control, so that it is not possible to blunder or sin, *none* of us is thus filled. Rather the filling of the Spirit is held out to us today as a *challenge*, a blessing of grace to be appropriated *by faith*. This is likewise true of every Christian virtue under the present dispensation of grace. Thus the apostle *exhorts* us:

"[Be] filled with the fruits of righteousness . . ." (Phil. 1:11).

"Be filled with the knowledge of His will . . ." (Col. 1:9).

"Be filled with the Spirit . . ." (Eph. 5:18).

None of us has as yet been *filled* with any of these, for in this present dispensation what God provides by grace we must appropriate by faith.[4] What a challenge!

JOHN'S ACCOUNT
JOHN 20:21-23

"As My Father hath sent Me, even so send I you."

The Father had sent our Lord to proclaim to Israel "the acceptable year of the Lord" (Luke 4:18, 19), and now He, in turn, sent the eleven to do the same ("even so send I you"), for the favored nation was to be given another opportunity to repent and turn to Christ (Luke 23:34; Acts 3:19-26). But Israel rejected the risen, ascended Christ as they had rejected Him while on earth. Thus they have been set aside as a nation, and judicially blinded. How, then,

---

4. For a more comprehensive discussion of this subject see the author's book, *True Spirituality*.

can our Lord's words "even so send I you" apply to *us* today? How, in the light of Rom. 11:7,25, and many similar passages regarding the (temporary) setting aside of Israel, can the so-called "great commission" possibly apply to *us?*

"Whose soever sins ye remit, they are remitted unto them; and whose soever sins ye retain, they are retained."

Though all the foregoing segments of the commission to the eleven should apply to us today—and none of them do—surely *this* part of the commission *could not possibly* apply to us. *None* of us are completely filled with, or controlled by, the Holy Spirit. *None* of us have the divine gift of knowledge. *None* of us are to represent our Lord officially as judges in His kingdom. How, then, are we in a position to remit sins? Thus obedience to this segment of the commission too has now been rendered *impossible.*

A Serious Side Effect

Chapter V

THE ATTEMPTED RECOVERY OF
THE SIGN GIFTS TODAY

A natural result of the confusion that prevails with regard to the so-called "great commission" is the attempted recovery of the sign gifts.

We have already shown that notwithstanding the claims made by many sincere believers, the commission to the eleven and the program of Pentecost *cannot* be carried out today. God has rendered this impossible, for the supernatural manifestations of that day have been *"done away"* and have *"ceased."* Hence the attempt to recover them is not of God but of Satan, who would use even the Scriptures to rob God's people of their most precious possessions.

SATAN AND THE SAINTS

As Satan used the Word of God itself to tempt our Lord, and used it again to cause the Galatians to "fall from grace" into the bondage of Moses' law, so he uses it in our day, pointing to the Scriptures themselves to draw sincere believers away from a full appreciation of "all spiritual blessings in the heavenlies" to the lesser blessings of a former dispensation. Our adversary is pleased when untaught Christians say: "If it's in the Bible it's enough for me," but there are two Scriptures he will never point men to: Rom. 11:13 and II Tim. 2:15, for were they heeded the theological confusion in the Church would be dispelled. All is clear when we "rightly divide the Word of truth."

It should be further observed that the attempted recovery of the sign gifts today is a distinct sign of *im*maturity. The sign gifts abounded in the Corinthian church (I Cor. 1:7 and Chaps. 12-14) and the Corinthians boasted of them, yet Paul let them know in no uncertain terms that they were mere "babes in Christ" (I Cor. 3:1) unable to digest solid food (I Cor. 3:2) and their "envying and strife and division" (I Cor. 3:3) proved that he was right.

In the light of this let no modern Pentecostalist imagine that his supposed "gifts" of healing or prophecy or tongues are signs of spirituality or maturity. The Corinthians had all these, yet were pronounced *carnal* rather than spiritual, *childish* rather than mature. The Pentecostal gifts in themselves were *never* an indication of spirituality. They were simply temporary *signs* associated with the *Messiahship* of our Lord. Certainly a visit to a Pentecostal meeting today should convince the thoughtful student of the Word that spiritual maturity is not one of their characteristics. A man rises to speak in an "unknown tongue." Another follows with an "interpretation." Or a "prophet" rises with some special "revelation" from the Lord. And what do they say? Do they offer some refreshing light on the Word, or discuss "the deep things of God"? No, they make such statements as: "The Lord is pleased with the meeting," or "The Lord is coming soon and we must be ready," or "There is a backslider in our midst and the Lord wants

89

him to know that if he doesn't soon seek God's face he will be cut off." And what brings the greatest response from the audience? The speaker who goes to the greatest extremes of physical or vocal exertion, the suggestion that the Holy Spirit is about to come down in power, or the mere mention of healing. But "the riches of the glory" of God's "mystery among the Gentiles," which God "would make known" to His saints (Col. 1:27) and by which believers are established (Rom. 16:25) is utterly unknown to them. In the words of another: "What they look upon as superior spirituality is actually instability and emotionalism that lasts only so long as the spell is upon them and then often drives them into a state of depression which is closely related to melancholia."

Referring to one who had embraced Pentecostalism and had been ruined by it, Sir Robert Anderson rightly said: "This complete surrender of mind and will—his entire personality—to what he believed to be the guidance of the Holy Spirit, left him a prey to the terrible delusions in which he was at last engulfed" (*Spirit Manifestations*, P. 19).

But the Corinthians had an exaggerated estimate of the value of the sign gifts at a time when they were at least in order. What shall we say of those who make much of them after God has suspended them and made them to cease? The surging waves of emotionalism, the constant emphasis on the miraculous, the self-deceit and the deception of others, the failure to recognize Paul as the God-appointed apostle of the present dispensation—all this is not of God, but of Satan.

90

CONVINCING MIRACLES

With convincing "signs and wonders" being wrought all about us in increasing numbers, some are being carried away from the truths so clearly set forth for our day in the epistles of Paul.

Some have concluded from these "supernatural manifestations" that toward the close of this present dispensation we may expect a revival of the divine gifts of tongues, healing, etc.

As to healing, may we first point out that no instructed believer in Pauline truth questions that God can, and often does, heal the sick and infirm as, for example, in the case of Epaphroditus (Phil. 2:25-27). We believe too that God is constantly working miracles. But we deny that *healers* and miracle *workers* or that *signs* and miraculous *demonstrations*, have any part in God's program for today.

First, the apostle did not say in I Cor. 13:8 that the gifts of prophecy, tongues and knowledge would be done away until the closing days of the dispensation. He simply declared that these miraculous manifestations were to be *done away* (i.e., in this new dispensation), and that "faith, hope and love" would "abide" (Ver. 13). Nor is there any indication in the Pauline epistles that the Pentecostal signs are to be restored at the close of this dispensation.

LYING WONDERS

The apostle does declare, however, that *after* the close of the dispensation of grace, the "man of sin" will appear "with all power and signs and *lying* wonders" (II Thes. 2:9). In this the apostle confirms what our Lord says in Matt. 24:24 about the same period of time:

"For there shall arise false Christs, and false prophets, and shall show great signs and wonders; insomuch that, if it were possible, they shall deceive the very elect."

During the "tribulation period," then, *after* the members of the Body of Christ have been "caught up" to be with the Lord, the ministers of Satan, from Antichrist down, will come with "all power and signs and lying wonders," to deceive, if possible, "the very elect."

But now let us see how this affects *us today*.

In the very same passage about Antichrist and his "power, and signs, and lying wonders," the apostle warns that

". . . the mystery of iniquity DOTH ALREADY WORK . . ." (II Thes. 2:7).

What does all this tell us about the multiplied "miracles" we are seeing all about us as the days grow darker: tongues, healing, prophecies, plus ESP, witchcraft, spiritism, exorcism, etc? Obviously it tells us that these are not of God, but of Satan.

We do not mean to imply that our Pentecostalist brethren would deceive us, but rather that Satan would deceive *them*.

A wondrous manifestation is to some the end of all argument. So-and-so must be of God or he could not work these miracles! But the above passages from the Bible tell us differently. Satan has power. He can work wonders, but he does so to deceive men and draw them away from the truth of God's glorious purpose and grace.

Indeed, Paul, in I Tim. 4:1, issues a stern warning to this effect:

"Now **THE SPIRIT SPEAKETH EXPRESSLY that in the latter times some shall depart from the faith,**[1] **GIVING HEED TO SEDUCING SPIRITS, AND DOCTRINES OF DEVILS [DEMONS]."**

This is one reason why the apostle urges all believers:

"Put on the whole armor of God, **THAT YE MAY BE ABLE TO STAND AGAINST THE WILES OF THE DEVIL.**

"FOR WE WRESTLE NOT AGAINST FLESH AND BLOOD, BUT AGAINST PRINCIPALITIES, AGAINST POWERS, AGAINST THE RULERS OF THE DARKNESS OF THIS WORLD, AGAINST SPIRITUAL WICKEDNESS [WICKED SPIRITS] IN HIGH [HEAVENLY] PLACES" (Eph. 6:11,12).

Be not deceived. Satan is not a grotesque creature with horns, hooves, a tail and a pitchfork. He inspired that caricature to draw attention *away* from himself, for when the apostle warns of *"false apostles, deceitful workers, transforming themselves into the apostles of Christ"* (II Cor. 11:13), he adds:

"And no marvel, for **SATAN HIMSELF IS TRANSFORMED INTO AN ANGEL OF LIGHT.**

"THEREFORE IT IS NO GREAT THING IF HIS MINISTERS ALSO BE TRANSFORMED AS THE MINISTERS OF RIGHTEOUSNESS . . ." (Vers. 14,15).

---

1. Obviously, "the faith" *he* had proclaimed, hence "the latter times" of *this "dispensation of the grace of God"* (Eph. 3:1-3).

There you have it! If Satan did appear as men portray him, the multitudes would flee from him. But *"an angel of light"* with *"ministers of righteousness"!* This attracts the unwary.

SATAN AND SICKNESS

But here is one who is stricken with some deadly disease. He is taken to a healing meeting and, seemingly at least, is completely restored. Can this possibly be of Satan?

Why not? Besides all his other powers, is it not he who *inflicts* sickness and disease? Think of the case of Job. Did not God permit Satan to bring Job to the point of death, physically (Job 2:4-9)? Think of Paul himself. Was it not "a messenger of Satan" who was sent to "buffet" him until he cried again and again for deliverance (II Cor. 12:7,8)? And is it not clearly stated in Heb. 2:14 that for the present Satan has *"the power of death"?*

If it is Satan, then, who inflicts sickness and disease, why cannot Satan *stop* inflicting them? Why can he not—why *would* he not, withdraw the illness he has inflicted upon you if this will cause you to center your interest on the wrong thing, and cause you to walk by sight, rather than by faith?

We specially mention bodily healing here because most people are attracted and convinced by this sort of supernatural demonstration. But the physical healings under our Lord's earthly ministry and at Pentecost were "signs." Signs of what? Signs of the validity of our Lord's royal claims. Had He

94

been accepted as King, all those thus healed would have gone into the prophesied kingdom, where sickness and disease would never again overtake them.

This is not so today, for the King and His kingdom have been rejected, and the reign of Christ on earth now awaits a future day. Thus it is that those who are "healed," all finally die like the rest. Though "healed" again and again, there always comes *that last time* when *nothing* avails.

One of the saddest aspects of modern healing campaigns is the long, sad trail of disillusionment and shaken faith it leaves behind. Some are not healed at all, and even those who are "healed" finally come to that last time, when Heb. 9:27 is fulfilled, for "it *is* appointed unto men once to die."

Again we say: What a list could be compiled of all those who once sincerely preached that it was a lack of faith, a sin, not to claim and expect from God a strong, sound body, yet they themselves all died.

How much better, then, to walk by faith and leave ourselves in His loving hands to do as He sees is best for us?

Thus we beg our Christian readers not to be carried away with amazing demonstrations that can only beguile us to take our eyes off *Him*. Rather let us heed the Spirit's exhortation through Paul:

"Be careful[2] for nothing; but in everything by prayer and supplication, with thanksgiving, let your requests be made known unto God.

---

2. I.e., full of care, anxious.

"AND THE PEACE OF GOD, WHICH PASSETH ALL UN-DERSTANDING, SHALL KEEP YOUR HEARTS AND MINDS THROUGH CHRIST JESUS" (Phil. 4:6,7).

PENTECOSTALISM AND SNAKES
ROMAN CATHOLICISM AND TONGUES

Never have we had more compelling evidence of the importance of "rightly dividing the Word of truth" than in this day of religious confusion.

Years ago the *Searchlight* published an article by the Editor titled, *The Great Commission and the Virginia Police*. At that time the question was: Do the Virginia Police have a legitimate right to stop Pentecostalists from handling snakes publicly? The law said they did, and the practice was soon discontinued.

Now, in 1974, however, snake-handling has again come to the fore, and it seems that this time the practice may be defended more ably—and all the way to the Supreme Court.

This writer saw and heard its chief proponent in America present his case before news reporters. "What if the law tells you that you *may not* handle snakes in public?" he was asked. "What will you do then?"

His answer was simple and to the point: "We always try to honor God by obeying the law, as He says we should. However, there are exceptions. When the law forbids us to follow God's specific instructions, we must obey the higher authority and say with Peter: 'We ought to obey God rather than men.' "

96

He then quoted the so-called "great commission" from Mark 16, including the phrase: *"They shall take up serpents"* (Ver. 18).

Asked if he had ever been bitten by snakes, he said, "Yes, seven times." Asked whether he had ever participated in snake-handling—or strychnine-drinking—episodes in which *others* had become ill or had died, he said, "Yes." Asked why he then persisted in the practice, he answered simply: "I don't blame the Lord for my lack of faith; I simply do what He told us to do in the 'great commission.' "

How the courts will rule in this case regarding freedom of religion vs. the public safety, we do not know, but meantime it is a rather frightening thing for the people of any community to learn that poisonous snakes will be let loose and freely handled in their communities.

We, of course, object to religious snake-handling on Scriptural as well as civil grounds, but what about the vast majority of our fundamentalist brethren?

Can any fundamentalist really find serious fault with those who handle snakes on the basis that this is included in the program outlined in the "great commission," when they themselves have taught for years that this commission, given by the Lord to His twelve apostles, is indeed *our* "great commission," the "marching orders" of the Church today? By what Scriptural rule can any believer *take what he wishes out of this commission* for his obedience, so that some use it to teach legalism (Matt. 28:20), others baptismal salvation (Mark 16:16), others speaking with tongues

97

(Ver. 17), others healing miracles (Ver. 18), still others absolution (John 20:21-23), or certain combinations of these, but none of them *all.*

If one fundamentalist believer can use this commission to teach water baptism, why should not another use it to teach snake-handling, for *this commission* distinctly says: *"These signs SHALL follow them that believe . . . they shall take up serpents. . . ."*

If the commission to the eleven is our commission, let's obey it *all.* It is not *our* prerogative to decide what part or parts of this commission we are to obey, and to ignore the rest. But if, in the light of a further revelation communicated by the glorified Lord to Paul, a new dispensation has been ushered in, let us hasten to acknowledge that the commission to the eleven is *not our commission.* The Church has not faced up to this challenge. This is the basic cause of the continued and growing confusion and division within its ranks.

But another startling phenomenon appearing on the religious horizon and growing fast is *Roman Catholic Pentecostalism.* Great numbers of Roman Catholic priests and people are involved in healing the sick, speaking in tongues, casting out demons, etc.

Here we ask, *Why not?* The Roman Church has always followed Peter rather than Paul, and has always taught that the "great commission" with its miraculous signs, its healing powers and its power to remit sins, is for our obedience. Only they, like others, chose what *they* felt would best further the

98

interests of Roman Catholicism and *de-emphasized* the rest.

Thus it is no great wonder that, with the charismatic movement growing like wildfire, Rome should now become interested in speaking with tongues, etc.

What an apostate system teaches, however, is not our chief concern. We are more deeply concerned about Bible-believing Christians, who are true to the fundamentals of the faith. Until these learn the importance of dispensational truth and begin to rightly divide God's Word, especially as to His message for the world today and His program for the Church today, they will be forced—self-forced—to go on serving the Lord as a divided army.

Chapter VI

WHAT THEN IS OUR COMMISSION?

We trust that it has now been made abundantly clear that the commission of our Lord to the eleven apostles, the so-called "great commission," is *not* the commission of the Church, the Body of Christ; it is *not* to be carried out today.

What then *is* our God-given commission? Before answering this let us consider briefly what happened to the commission given to the eleven.

We have emphasized the fact that the so-called "great commission" and the prophetic program in general were *interrupted.* The apostles and disciples *could not* carry out their commission *to its completion* due to Israel's stubborn rejection of Messiah. But after it had become evident that Jerusalem and the favored nation would not repent and receive Messiah, the leaders of the twelve agreed, under the guidance of the Holy Spirit, to confine their ministry to Israel alone while others went to the Gentiles. We will discuss this later in detail, but first:

PROPHECY INTERRUPTED
THE MYSTERY REVEALED

When Peter arose to speak at Pentecost to explain the gift of tongues, he declared that the last days had come (Acts 2:16,17) and that this would be further evidenced by two phenomena: (1) the pouring out of the Spirit on God's people and, (2) the pouring out of judgment upon His enemies, all prophesied by Joel with regard to *"that great and terrible day of the Lord"* (Acts 2:14-21; cf., Joel 2:28-32).

As we know, the Spirit *was* "poured out," but not the judgments that were to bring in the day of the Lord. There were no "wonders in heaven above" or "blood" or "fire" or "vapor of smoke." The sun was not "turned into darkness," nor the moon "into blood."

Rather, when Israel rejected the apostles' offer of the return of Christ and "the times of refreshing"; when the stage was all set, as it were, for the judgment to fall, God did a wonderful thing.

In an amazing act of grace, the rejected Lord reached down from heaven, *not* to crush Saul of Tarsus, the leader of the rebellion, but to *save* him and make him His own apostle of grace, thus ushering in the present "dispensation of the grace of God."

It was to this *other* apostle that God committed the glorious message and program which is ours today. Stated briefly, it was that God would now reconcile believing Jews and Gentiles to Himself by grace through faith, apart from the law or works, all on the basis of the blood shed at Calvary for the remission of sins. Those who accepted this offer of reconciliation and thus became members of the "one body," were to be given a heavenly position and prospect,

101

and "all spiritual blessings in the heavenlies in Christ." The most general term for all this good news is, *"the gospel of the grace of God,"* which the Apostle Paul declared, in Acts 20:24, had been specifically committed to him.

The prophetic Scriptures, of course, contained no hint of all this. It was "a mystery hid in God," "hid from ages and from generations," and "kept secret since the world [or *ages*] began" (Eph. 3:9; Col. 1:26; Rom. 16:25). This is why the apostle again and again calls this great body of truth, "the mystery," or "the secret."

OUR GREAT COMMISSION

Where the lost are concerned, then, our commission comprises an offer of *reconciliation* to God through the death of Christ. This could hardly be stated more clearly than it is in II Cor. 5:14-21:

"For the love of Christ constraineth us; because we thus judge, that if one died for all, then were all dead:

"And that He died for all, that they which live should not henceforth live unto themselves, but unto Him which died for them, and rose again.

"Wherefore, HENCEFORTH KNOW WE NO MAN AFTER THE FLESH: YEA THOUGH WE HAVE KNOWN CHRIST AFTER THE FLESH, YET NOW HENCEFORTH KNOW WE HIM NO MORE.

"Therefore IF ANY MAN BE IN CHRIST HE IS A NEW CREATURE [Lit., "there is a new creation"]: OLD THINGS ARE PASSED AWAY; BEHOLD, ALL THINGS ARE BECOME NEW.

102

"AND ALL THINGS ARE OF GOD,[1] WHO HATH RECON-CILED US TO HIMSELF BY JESUS CHRIST, AND HATH GIVEN TO US THE MINISTRY OF RECONCILIATION;

"To wit, that God was in Christ, reconciling the world unto Himself, not imputing their trespasses unto them; and HATH COMMITTED UNTO US THE WORD OF RECONCILIATION.

"Now then we are ambassadors for Christ, as though God did beseech you by us, we pray you in Christ's stead be ye reconciled to God.

"For He hath made Him to be sin for us, [Him] who knew no sin; that we might be made the righteousness of God in Him."

How tempted we are to go into an exposition of this passage, but we merely quote it here to show that God "hath given to us *the ministry of reconciliation*," and "hath COMMITTED unto us the word of reconciliation." *This* is *our* "GREAT COMMIS-SION," the proclamation of the greatest message ever sent by God to man.

Under this commission we are no longer to differ-entiate between Jew and Gentile for "henceforth know we no man after the flesh." Nor are we even to know Christ after the flesh for, "now henceforth know we *Him* [Christ after the flesh] no more" (Ver. 16). Rather the Apostle Paul prays most earnestly that we might know Him as the One "*far above all principality, and power, and might, and dominion, and every name that is named, not only in this world, but also in that which is to come*" (Eph. 1:21).

---

1. I.e., in this new dispensation *all is of God*. There are no sacrifices, no feast days, no baptism; nothing for man to do to gain acceptance with Him. Salvation is by simple faith in what *He* has done for us.

103

It should be noted here that whereas the twelve had never seen Christ *in heaven* (At His ascension "a cloud received Him *out of their sight*" — Acts 1:9.), Paul had never seen Christ *on earth* (I Cor. 15:8). This was appropriate in view of the difference in their ministries. The twelve had been sent to proclaim the *return* of Christ to reign *on earth*, while Paul was later sent to proclaim the *grace* of Christ and His headship over the Body, with its *heavenly* calling and position.

Under Paul's commission, and ours, we are to require nothing for salvation but simple faith in the One who was "made sin for us that we might be made the righteousness of God in Him" (II Cor. 5:21). Indeed, rather than demanding anything of the lost we are to "pray" *them*, to earnestly *beseech* them, "in Christ's stead," to be "reconciled to God" (Ver. 20). *This is infinite grace indeed!*

Finally, obedience to *this* great commission brings believing Jews and Gentiles alike into a "new creation": *"Therefore if any man be in Christ, he is* [Lit., *there is*] *a new creation"* (Cf., Eph. 2:10; 4:24; Col. 3:10).

Mark well, *this*, says the inspired apostle, is *our* great commission.

"GOD . . . HATH GIVEN TO US THE MINISTRY OF RECONCILIATION" (Ver. 18).

"GOD . . . HATH COMMITTED UNTO US THE WORD OF RECONCILIATION" (Ver. 19).

Let the Church once recognize *this* glorious commission as distinctively hers, and the major cause of denominational division will be removed.

God grant that the walls of denominationalism may soon tumble and fall, at least for His people, and that they may proclaim to the world with one voice:

"NOW THEN WE ARE AMBASSADORS FOR CHRIST, AS THOUGH GOD DID BESEECH YOU BY US: WE PRAY YOU IN CHRIST'S STEAD, BE YE RECONCILED TO GOD.

"FOR HE HATH MADE HIM TO BE SIN FOR US, [HIM] WHO KNEW NO SIN; THAT WE MIGHT BE MADE THE RIGHTEOUSNESS OF GOD IN HIM."

THE COMMISSION TO THE ELEVEN SUPERSEDED BY THE COMMISSION TO PAUL

Surely no one even superficially acquainted with the Book of Acts and the Epistles of Paul will question the fact that sometime *after* our Lord's commission to the eleven, *Paul* was sent, as an apostle of Christ, to proclaim to all mankind "*the gospel of the grace of God.*"

The question, however, is whether Paul was sent out under a different commission from that to the eleven; whether his was a *different message* from theirs, and whether this constituted *a change in commission.* This is answered for us in many passages in Paul's epistles, but especially in Gal. 2:1-9.

Here he relates how he went up to Jerusalem again, and this time, he says, "[I] took Titus with me also." As we consider the passage further we shall see the significance of this statement. Here, however, it is noteworthy that the apostle adds that he went up to Jerusalem on this occasion "by revelation," i.e., the Lord instructed him to go. Why? This is answered for us in the rest of the sentence:

". . . and [I] communicated unto them THAT GOSPEL WHICH I PREACH AMONG THE GENTILES, BUT PRIVATELY TO THEM WHICH WERE OF REPUTATION, LEST BY ANY MEANS I SHOULD RUN, OR HAD RUN, IN VAIN" (Ver. 2).

In the light of this passage, how futile to argue that Paul merely went up to check with the other apostles to make sure he was preaching the same message as they!

First, he had been *sent* up to Jerusalem by the Lord *because* believers *from Judaea* had sought to impose circumcision and the law upon the Gentile believers (Acts 15:1,2). *Second,* he states that he "communicated" to the leaders at Jerusalem *"that gospel which I preach among the Gentiles."* This phraseology is common to Paul's epistles, indicating that *"that gospel"* which he preached to the Gentiles was *not* the same as the gospel which the apostles at Jerusalem had been preaching to the people of Israel. *Third,* this is further confirmed by the fact that in communicating this information to the leaders at Jerusalem he first went *"privately* to them which were of reputation." Why should he have to do this if his message was the same as that which they were preaching at Jerusalem? He was obviously trying to convince them of the truth and validity of "that gospel" which he had been preaching among the Gentiles.

106

This all being so, it was important to the apostle to have Titus, a Gentile, with him as a test case, for in Verse 3 he says:

"But neither Titus, who was with me, being a Greek, was compelled to be circumcised."

Note the word "compelled." Some would have intimidated or coerced Titus into subjecting himself to circumcision and the law, but Titus, like Paul, was a man of strong, godly character and Paul says, as it were: "And they didn't compel Titus, the Gentile, to be circumcised either!" And then, referring to certain "false brethren unawares brought in," who had sought "privily to spy out" the Gentiles' liberty in Christ, he declares:

"To whom we gave place by subjection, no, not for an hour; that the truth of the gospel might continue with you" (Ver. 5).

All this makes it clear that "that gospel" which Paul preached among the Gentiles was a *new* revelation, never before made known. And if this be not enough we have a statement in Verses 7-9 that proves beyond a doubt that Paul's commission superseded that of the eleven. Here we read that *"they saw* that the gospel of the uncircumcision was committed unto me [Paul] as the gospel of the circumcision was unto Peter."

"And when James, Cephas [Peter] and John . . . PERCEIVED the grace that was given unto me [Paul], THEY GAVE TO ME AND BARNABAS THE RIGHT HANDS OF FELLOWSHIP; THAT WE SHOULD GO UNTO THE HEATHEN, AND THEY UNTO THE CIRCUMCISION" (Ver. 9).

Here, by a solemn, official agreement, Peter, James and John promise to confine their ministry

107

to Israel while Paul goes to the Gentiles. This is striking in view of the fact that the twelve, not Paul, had originally been sent into all the world.

Were they all out of the will of God in making this agreement? By no means! Subsequent revelation proves that they were all very much in the will of God and that Israel's rejection of Christ had brought about a change in the program.

Thus the leaders at Jerusalem "loosed" themselves, under the leading of the Holy Spirit, from the commission under which they had at first been sent, and what they "loosed on earth" was indeed "loosed in heaven" (Matt. 18:18).

Had not the eleven been sent into *all the world*," to "make disciples of all nations"? Did not this include the Gentiles? Yet here they acknowledge *Paul* as the apostle to the Gentiles, at the same time agreeing that they are to *discontinue* the pursuance of their earlier commission to evangelize all the world. How can anyone read this, simply *read* it, and question the fact that to Paul was given a special commission and that this superseded, historically, the commission given to the eleven?

This passage alone should be sufficient to convince those who still wish to carry out the so-called "great commission," that this is now *impossible*. It was given up long ago as God raised up that *other* apostle, Paul, and committed to him that message which has brought salvation and blessing to millions down through the centuries since.

PAUL AND HIS COMMISSION

It is significant that the three terms employed in the so-called "great commission" to indicate its world-wide scope, are also used in Paul's epistles in connection with his ministry. Only, whereas the twelve never got to *"all nations," "all the world"* or *"all creation"* with their message, Paul *did* with his.

In closing his epistle to the Romans the apostle says:

"Now to Him that is of power to stablish you according to my gospel, and the preaching of Jesus Christ according to the revelation of the mystery, which was kept secret since the world began.

"BUT NOW IS MADE MANIFEST, AND by the scriptures of the prophets,[2] according to the commandment of the everlasting God, MADE KNOWN TO ALL NATIONS for the obedience of faith" (Rom. 16:25,26).

And to the Colossians he writes concerning *"the truth of the gospel"*:

"WHICH IS COME UNTO YOU, AS IT IS IN ALL THE WORLD; and bringeth forth fruit, as it doth also in you . . ." (Col. 1:6).

". . . which ye have heard, and WHICH WAS PREACHED TO EVERY CREATURE WHICH IS UNDER HEAVEN [or ALL CREATION UNDER HEAVEN]; whereof I Paul am made a minister" (Col. 1:23).

Various arguments may be advanced to prove that "the gospel of the grace of God" did not actually reach "all the world" or "all creation," and we do not deny that to those addressed "all the

---

2. Lit., *prophetic writings,* i.e., his own writings, for it had been *"kept secret"* and was only *"now"* made manifest.

world" would doubtless mean all the *known* world, and "all creation" would likewise mean all the creation *as they knew it*. But the point is that whatever these three phrases mean in the so-called "great commission," they must also mean in these statements by Paul, for the terms are exactly identical in the original.

We have seen how the twelve did *not* get their message to "all nations," "all the world," or "all creation," because, on the one hand Israel rejected it and on the other hand God had a secret purpose to unfold. But Paul, to whom this secret purpose was revealed, says that by the grace of God he *did* get *his* message to "all nations," "all the world" and "all creation."

Whereas the twelve never got beyond their own nation in carrying out their commission, it is written of Paul that during his stay at Ephesus *"all they which dwelt in Asia* [in Asia Minor] *heard the word of the Lord Jesus"* (Acts 19:10). To the Romans he writes: *"from Jerusalem, and round about unto Illyricum, I have fully preached the gospel of Christ"* (Rom. 15:19), and speaks of his plans to go to Spain (15:24), plans which were probably accomplished between his two imprisonments. Even of his helpers it was said: *"These that have turned the world upside down are come hither also"* (Acts 17:6). And to the Romans again he says: *"your faith is spoken of throughout the whole world"* (Rom. 1:8).

With regard to this last statement it is argued

110

by some that since Paul had not even been to Rome by then, it must be that believers from the Jerusalem Church had gotten as far as Rome under their "great commission."

We do not accept this as valid, for while indeed there were "strangers from Rome" present at Pentecost, there is no indication that there was any substantial number of these, or that those present were even converted, much less that they started a church at Rome. On the other hand we do read in Acts 8:1 that in the great persecution in Jerusalem "they were all scattered abroad throughout *the regions of Judaea and Samaria*, except the apostles." Then, with regard to this same scattering we read further:

"Now they which were scattered abroad upon the persecution that arose about Stephen travelled AS FAR AS Phenice, and Cyprus, and Antioch, preaching the Word to none but unto THE JEWS ONLY.

"And SOME of them were men of Cyprus and Cyrene, which, when they were come to ANTIOCH, spake UNTO THE GREEKS,[3] preaching the Lord Jesus" (Acts 11:19,20).

When the Church at Jerusalem heard of this they sent Barnabas to look into it and *he* went to Tarsus to find *Saul*, and under Saul the Church at Antioch became the base of operations for the evangelization of the *Gentiles* with "the gospel of the grace of God."

It was from Antioch that, as we have seen, Paul went by revelation to Jerusalem to communicate to

---

3. Not *Grecians,* for Grecians were *Jews,* and this would have been nothing unusual.

111

the leaders there that gospel which he preached among the Gentiles (Gal. 2:2), with the result that they promised to confine their ministry to Israel, official-ly and publicly recognizing *Paul* as the apostle of the Gentiles (Ver. 9). And even *at that council*, the Cir-cumcision apostles wrote concerning those who had gone out from them to impose their message and pro-gram upon the Gentiles:

"Forasmuch as we have heard, that **CERTAIN WHICH WENT OUT FROM US** have troubled you with words, subverting your souls, saying, Ye must be circumcised, and keep the law: **TO WHOM WE GAVE NO SUCH COMMANDMENT**" (Acts 15:24).

The Circumcision saints themselves still re-mained under the law for the time being (see Acts 21:20) but, recognizing Paul's further revelation and his commission to the Gentiles, they condemned as trouble-makers those of their number who sought to impose their message and program upon the Gentiles. And Paul also called them trouble-makers (Gal. 1:6,7).

Thus those to whom Paul wrote at Rome could scarcely have been converts of the Circumcision be-lievers at Jerusalem. They had doubtless been won to Christ through those whom Paul had reached with "the gospel of the grace of God."

This leads us to recognize another important fact. We have seen from Matt. 24:14 that if the twelve had gotten their message to all the world, "the end" of that dispensation would have come. This proves at the same time that Paul was *not* la-boring to fulfill that "great commission" and that he did *not* preach the same gospel as they, for then

112

"the end" would have come in his day, since he *says* that *his* message *had* gone to "all nations" and "all the world."

THE AMAZING ENERGY WITH WHICH PAUL PROCLAIMED GRACE

To the Romans the apostle writes of his commission from the ascended Lord:

"By whom we have received grace and apostleship, for obedience to the faith among ALL NATIONS, for His name" (Rom. 1:5).

In his Epistle to the Ephesians he writes:

"Unto me, who am less than the least of all saints, is this grace given, that I should preach among the Gentiles the unsearchable riches of Christ;

"And TO MAKE ALL MEN SEE what is the fellowship [or, dispensation] of the mystery . . ." (Eph. 3:8,9).

But while it is generally acknowledged that he was *commissioned* to proclaim grace to all nations, there are few who have quite realized the amazing energy with which the apostle proclaimed this message in the face of the most relentless persecution, or the wide extent of his ministry and influence.

In Pisidian Antioch *"almost the whole city"* came together to hear the Word of God, but the unbelieving Jews, filled with envy, contradicted and blasphemed, and it was necessary for Paul and Barnabas to turn from them to the Gentiles.

"And the Word of the Lord was published throughout all the region.

"But the Jews stirred up the devout and honorable women, and the chief men of the city, and raised persecution against

113

Paul and Barnabas, and expelled them out of their coasts" (Acts 13:49,50).

In Iconium, where he next preached the gospel, *"the multitude of the city was divided,"*

"And when there was an assault made both of the Gentiles, and also of the Jews with their rulers, to use them despitefully, and to stone them,

"They were ware of it, and fled to Lystra and Derbe. . . .

"And there they preached the gospel" (Acts 14:5-7).

At Lystra the people first tried to offer sacrifices to Paul and Barnabas as gods, but this attitude changed abruptly when

". . . there came thither certain Jews from Antioch and Iconium, who persuaded the people, and, having stoned Paul, drew [dragged] him out of the city supposing he had been dead" (Acts 14:19).

And then, after preaching the gospel in Derbe, and teaching many, they went right back to the cities where they had risked their lives and had suffered such persecution.

"Confirming the souls of the disciples, and exhorting them to continue in the faith . . ." (Acts 14:22).

Returning to Antioch in Syria, from whence they had been sent forth, they found certain men from Judaea seeking to bring the Gentile believers under the law of Moses, and *"Paul and Barnabas had no small dissension and disputation with them"* (Acts 15:2).

As a result of this Paul and Barnabas went up to Jerusalem to settle the matter with the leaders of the Messianic Church there. On this occasion, as we have seen, Paul took Titus, a Greek, with him as a test case and was later able to write to the Galatians: *"Titus . . . was not compelled to be circumcised either."* And concerning those who would have had it so, he said:

"To whom we gave place by subjection, no, not for an hour; that the truth of the gospel might continue with you" (Gal. 2:5).

Think of the energy required for all this!

Next we find the apostle going forth with Silas and again it is peril, persecution and toil wherever he goes.

At Philippi he is beaten with many stripes and imprisoned. At Thessalonica *"the Jews which believed not . . . set all the city on an uproar"* (Acts 17:5) and things became so dangerous that *"the brethren immediately sent away Paul and Silas by night unto Berea"* (Ver. 10). But the unbelieving Jews from Thessalonica followed him to Berea and *"stirred up the people"* there, so that this time *"the brethren sent away Paul to go as it were to the sea,"* but actually *"brought him unto Athens"* (Acts 17:13-15).

At Athens he got "the cold shoulder" and *"departed from among them"* to Corinth, where he was able to remain for a year and six months, but not without tasting much opposition and persecution (I Cor. 2:3; Acts 18:9,10,12,13).

At Ephesus he went to the synagogue *"and spake boldly for the space of three months, disputing and persuading the things concerning the kingdom* of God." Then, when "divers were hardened, and believed not" he "separated the disciples" from the unbelieving multitude and went with them to "the school of one Tyrannus," where he "disputed daily."

"And this continued by the space of two years; so that all they which dwelt in Asia[4] heard the word of the Lord Jesus, both Jews and Greeks" (Acts 19:8-10).

Indeed, before Paul left Ephesus so much had been accomplished that a spontaneous public bonfire was held, at which the occult leaders who had been won to Christ burned their pagan books, amounting in value to 50,000 pieces of silver. "So mightily grew the Word of God and prevailed" (Acts 19:20). But this was followed by the great uproar at which Demetrius and the craftsmen who made silver shrines for Diana stirred up the unbelieving masses to such a pitch that for two hours they cried, "Great is Diana of the Ephesians" (Ver. 34).

"And when Paul would have entered in unto the people, the disciples suffered him not" (Ver. 30).

Concerning this ministry in Asia Minor the apostle writes to the Corinthians:

"For we would not, brethren, have you ignorant of our trouble which came to us in Asia; that WE WERE PRESSED OUT OF MEASURE, ABOVE STRENGTH, INSOMUCH THAT WE DESPAIRED EVEN OF LIFE" (II Cor. 1:8).

At Troas, on the first day of the week, Paul preached in an upper room "until midnight" (Acts 20:7), then "talked a long while, even till the break of

---

4. A province of Asia Minor.

day" (Ver. 11) and *then* departed again to continue his journey to Jerusalem. Think of it!

"And from Miletus he sent to Ephesus, and called for the elders of the church" and, exhorting them to stand fast, reminded them how he had served the Lord among them, *". . . with many tears, and temptations, which befell me by the lying in wait of the Jews: and . . . taught you publicly and from house to house"* (Vers. 17-20), adding:

"Therefore watch and remember, that BY THE SPACE OF THREE YEARS I CEASED NOT TO WARN EVERY ONE NIGHT AND DAY WITH TEARS" (Ver. 31).

Finally, having been sent from Jerusalem to Rome in chains he was able to write to the Philippian believers:

". . . the things which happened unto me have fallen out rather unto the furtherance of the gospel;

"So that MY BONDS IN CHRIST ARE MANIFEST IN ALL THE PALACE, AND IN ALL OTHER PLACES" (Phil. 1:12,13).

And again:

". . . The brethren which are with me greet you.

"ALL THE SAINTS SALUTE YOU, CHIEFLY THEY THAT ARE OF CAESAR'S HOUSEHOLD" (Phil. 4:21,22).

So mightily was the apostle used, even while in bonds, that his imprisonment for Christ was a subject of discussion throughout and beyond wicked Nero's palace, and a company of believers had sprung up within the palace itself.

All the while the apostle continued, in the face of much opposition, to do his utmost to get the truth to those without, even to those whom he had never seen, writing letters to them which still thrill the hearts of millions today.

His words to the Colossian believers reflect the earnest effort that the apostle, even now, was putting into the ministry committed to him:

"FOR I WOULD THAT YE KNEW WHAT GREAT CONFLICT I HAVE FOR YOU, AND FOR THEM AT LAODICEA, AND FOR AS MANY AS HAVE NOT SEEN MY FACE IN THE FLESH.

"THAT THEIR HEARTS MIGHT BE COMFORTED, BEING KNIT TOGETHER IN LOVE, AND UNTO ALL RICHES OF THE FULL ASSURANCE OF UNDERSTANDING, TO THE ACKNOWLEDGMENT OF THE MYSTERY OF GOD, AND OF THE FATHER, AND OF CHRIST" (Col. 2:1,2).

Thus, under Paul's ministry there did take place a world-wide proclamation of "the gospel of the grace of God," so that he could write to Titus about the *epiphany,* the shining forth, of God's grace to all mankind (Tit. 2:11).

THE APOSTLE DIVINELY EMPOWERED

But even recognizing Paul's organized efforts to send the gospel to "the regions beyond," how could one man have accomplished so much? What was the source of the amazing energy that took him from one uprising into another; that urged him on and on with his proclamation of the gospel of grace, though even lacking much-needed rest? How could he keep enduring stripes and imprisonments, stonings and shipwrecks, long journeys with perils of every sort? How could he go on bearing weariness, pain, watchings, hunger, thirst, cold, nakedness? And all these he had already suffered by the time he wrote his Second Epistle to the Corinthians—in addition to *"the care of all the churches"* (II Cor. 11:23-28). Indeed, in his First Epistle to the Corinthians he writes:

"Even unto this present hour we both hunger, and thirst, and are naked, and are buffeted, and have no certain dwelling place" (I Cor. 4:11).

How could one man endure all this?

The answer to this question is given to us in the inspired writings of the apostle himself. It is simply that he was *divinely empowered,* as the following passages indicate:

"BUT BY THE GRACE OF GOD I AM WHAT I AM: AND HIS GRACE WHICH WAS BESTOWED UPON ME WAS NOT IN VAIN; BUT I LABORED MORE ABUNDANTLY THAN THEY ALL: YET NOT I, BUT THE GRACE OF GOD WHICH WAS WITH ME" (I Cor. 15:10).

"FOR HE THAT WROUGHT EFFECTUALLY IN PETER TO THE APOSTLESHIP OF THE CIRCUMCISION, THE SAME WAS MIGHTY IN ME TOWARD THE GENTILES" (Gal. 2:8).

"Whereunto I also labor, STRIVING ACCORDING TO HIS WORKING, WHICH WORKETH IN ME MIGHTILY" (Col. 1:29).

"At my first answer [before Nero] no man stood with me, but all men forsook me: I pray God that it may not be laid to their charge.

"NOTWITHSTANDING THE LORD STOOD WITH ME, AND STRENGTHENED ME; THAT BY ME THE PREACHING MIGHT BE FULLY KNOWN, AND THAT ALL THE GEN-TILES MIGHT HEAR: and I was delivered out of the mouth of the lion" (II Tim. 4:16,17).

Thus it was that the apostle could write about *"the epiphany of grace,"* the shining forth of grace, *"to all mankind."*

119

THE LIGHT DIMMED

But alas how the light has since been dimmed! How lightly men have esteemed the infinite grace of God! Indeed, it was during the apostle's own ministry that he had to write to the Galatians:

"I MARVEL THAT YE ARE SO SOON REMOVED FROM HIM THAT CALLED YOU INTO THE GRACE OF CHRIST UNTO ANOTHER GOSPEL" (Gal. 1:6).

For this Christendom has called the Galatian believers fickle, and commentators have quoted the statements of certain Roman rulers to prove that the Gauls were by nature changeable. We believe, however, that politicians and statesmen in any age, including our own, could be cited to prove that the public is fickle! Certainly the Apostle Paul would have to say with respect to the Church as a whole, historically: *"I marvel that ye are so soon removed from him that called you into the grace of Christ unto another gospel."*

Galatians 1:6 is not only the word of Paul to the Galatians; it is also the Word of God to the Church as a whole, for how soon the Church departed from the great revelation of the glorified Christ through Paul! This declension *began*, as we say, during Paul's own lifetime. One church after another was affected by it. We have seen how through his ministry "all they which dwelt in Asia heard the word of the Lord Jesus," but it was not many years before the apostle had to write to Timothy:

"THIS THOU KNOWEST, THAT ALL THEY WHICH ARE IN ASIA BE TURNED AWAY FROM ME . . ." (II Tim. 1:15).

120

From the writings of the early-century fathers which still exist, it is evident that rather than recognizing the distinctive character of Paul's message, they had it all confused with the kingdom message proclaimed by John the Baptist, Christ and the twelve, even to requiring water baptism for the remission of sins. And this declension went on apace until the Dark Ages, when Rome held sway and a mixture of Christianity, Judaism and heathen idolatry prevailed.

OUR RESPONSIBILITY TO RELIGHT THE TORCH

Years later the Church *began* to emerge from the darkness and superstition of Romanism as Luther, Zwingli, Calvin and others were raised up to recover Pauline truth. And, thank God, still greater advances were made under such men as Darby and Scofield, and later, J. C. O'Hair. But much, very much, still remains to be done. Those of us who are now laboring to carry out the commission of the glorified Lord *to us*, who desire to recover and make known the blessed message of grace and glory, will have to pray and toil and sacrifice as never before to make any impression upon the indifferent masses—including carnal Christians. Those Christian leaders who know the truth but maintain a discreet silence because they fear men or "love the praise of men," yes, and those who fail to proclaim the *whole* truth for "diplomacy's sake"—all these will have to cast aside their selfish interests if the grace of God is to shine forth with any degree of brightness again.

We know, of course, that the millennium will be brought in *by the return of Christ*, not by the efforts of men. But we have not been discussing the millennium. We have been discussing God's revealed program for "this present evil age," the time of Christ's rejection and absence, and it is God's *command* that we make the message of His grace known to all men. The fact that "evil men and seducers shall wax worse and worse" does not relieve us of this responsibility. However the darkness may deepen, we are to *"shine as lights in the world; holding forth the Word of life"* (Phil. 2:15,16).

As we have seen, God's grace was once made to shine forth to all mankind in spite of the most bitter and Satanic opposition. Then the torch began to flicker until the world was plunged into the Dark Ages and scarcely a spark remained. Then, after centuries, it was lit again and began to burn somewhat more brightly. But still it must be made to blaze afar.

In these critical times shall we not make it *our one passion* to *know* God's Word, rightly divided, and to *make it known* to others, until the grace of God shines forth again as a blazing torch? Shall we not, *must* we not, put aside *every* other consideration and say with Paul:

"BUT AS WE [ARE] ALLOWED OF GOD TO BE PUT IN TRUST WITH THE GOSPEL, EVEN SO WE SPEAK; NOT AS PLEASING MEN, BUT GOD, WHICH TRIETH OUR HEARTS" (I Thes. 2:4).

Soon enough our Lord will appear in glory and our work will be done. *Now* He would have us "buy up the time" and use our God-given energies to make known His *grace* to all who will hear.

Chapter VII

A RULE TO REMEMBER

For many years the Rule Book of the *Union Pacific Railroad* contained—and possibly it still does—the following important directive:

"Unless otherwise provided, train orders once in effect continue so until fulfilled, superseded or annulled."

This directive can be found, in essence, not only in the rule books of other railroads, but in the manuals of the various branches of our armed forces. This must be so, for where there is no discipline there is confusion.

This is particularly true where God's instructions to His people are concerned. These too remain in force until fulfilled, superseded or annulled, and the curse of confusion inevitably results when this divine rule is violated.

This brings us to the question: What *are* God's instructions for the fulfillment of His purposes *in our day?*

As we have seen, the great majority of professing Christians hold that our Lord's last orders, and those which we are to carry out today, are to be found in His commission to the eleven before His ascension to heaven. By almost common consent this commission has been called "the great commission." We, however, dissent from this view and maintain that it is this mistake which lies at the root of the confusion and division which have gripped the Church in our day.

Those who teach that we should labor under this commission do not themselves *obey* it. *They do not teach their hearers to observe all that our Lord commanded during His earthly ministry. They do not sell their possessions and distribute the proceeds to the poor. They do not send their missionaries out without provision. They do not attend synagogues on the sabbath day or offer the sacrifices of the ceremonial law.* Comparatively few of them require water baptism for salvation or hold that miraculous signs are the evidences of salvation. And surely, outside of the Church of Rome, few claim to remit sins.

But the twelve apostles and the "little flock" of Messiah's followers *did begin* to carry out this commission as we have seen. They *did* sell their belongings and distribute to the needy. They *did* go forth without material provisions, so that Peter, their leader, could say, "Silver and gold have I *NONE*." They practically lived in the temple and strictly observed the ceremonial law. They required repentance *and* water baptism for the remission of sins, and miraculous signs *did* follow those who believed. Read the early chapters of Acts and observe how meticulously they obeyed their "great commission."

124

But Israel would not heed their message or accept Jesus as Messiah, so the apostles were unable to fulfil their commission or to make disciples of all nations. Since Israel refused to accept Christ, therefore, this "great commission" was brought to a standstill. It could not, for the present, be fulfilled. This is not to imply that it has been annulled, for in Matt. 24:14 we read concerning a future day:

"And this gospel of the kingdom shall be preached in all the world for a witness to all nations; and then shall the end come."

But while the commission to the eleven has neither been fulfilled nor annulled, we have demonstrated from the Scriptures that for this present dispensation it has been *superseded* by the issuing of *other* orders, those which our glorified Lord committed by revelation to that *other* apostle, *Paul.*

OUR GREAT COMMISSION
NEITHER FULFILLED
NOR SUPERSEDED NOR ANNULLED

In Gal. 1:11,12 the Apostle Paul uses phraseology that is typical of his epistles. He uses the phrase, *"the gospel which was preached of [by] me,"* and explains why, saying:

"I certify you, brethren, that the gospel which was preached of me is not after man.

"For I neither received it of man, neither was I taught it, but by the revelation of Jesus Christ."

To the twelve had been committed the preaching of Jesus Christ *according to covenant and prophecy,* while Paul was later sent forth to proclaim "the preaching of Jesus Christ *according to the revelation of the mystery*," which had been "*kept secret since the world began.*" This message he calls "*my gospel,*" to distinguish it from that which the twelve had previously been preaching (See Rom. 16:25).

Both Peter and Paul referred to the crucifixion in their preaching, but whereas Peter *charged* his hearers with the crucifixion of Christ and called upon them to repent of this evil deed, Paul proclaimed the *glad news* that Christ's death was *our* death, the complete payment for our sins—sins that would have banished us forever from the presence of God. Both proclaimed the resurrection, but Peter *warned* men that God had raised Christ from the dead to sit on the throne of David, Israel's rebellion notwithstanding, while Paul associated it with our justification and our resurrection to "newness of life." This is why Paul exhorts Timothy:

"Consider what I say, and the Lord give thee understanding in all things.

"Remember that Jesus Christ, of the seed of David, was raised from the dead according to my gospel" (II Tim. 2:7,8).

Again, both Peter and Paul referred to the ascension, but Peter *warned* those who had participated in the crucifixion of Christ that He had ascended to the Father's right hand *until His enemies should be made His footstool* (Acts 2:35) while Paul declared that He was seated in heaven in the satisfaction of an accomplished redemption and as Head of the Body, the Church of today.

So, both Peter and Paul preached *Christ*, for "*other foundation can no man lay,*" but what a glorious advance Paul's message was over that which Peter and the eleven had proclaimed at Pentecost! And thus the so-called "great commission" has been superseded by another and greater commission entrusted to Paul and to us.

Since this greatest of all commissions has never been *fulfilled, nor superseded, nor annulled,* it remains in force today and we are responsible before God to obey it.

The Necessary Equipment

Chapter VIII

LIGHT AND POWER
TO FULFIL OUR COMMISSION

We have seen that the twelve apostles did not understand the prophetic program, indeed, that it was "hid from them" (Luke 9:45; 18:34), until our Lord, at a given moment "opened . . . their understanding, that they might understand the Scriptures" (Luke 24:45). We have seen too that at a given moment, "when the day of Pentecost was fully come," God fulfilled a long-standing promise and the apostles and disciples "were all filled with the Holy Spirit" (Acts 2:1,4).

This, however, is not how believers today are enlightened and empowered to proclaim "the mystery" since revealed through Paul. God does not at some given time miraculously open our eyes to understand the Scriptures. Rather the understanding of the Word comes through diligent, prayerful study, and with a fuller understanding comes the needed power.

Thus the apostle prayed for himself and for all saints, that they might be given the grace to understand and might thus be empowered to proclaim the glorious message committed to him. Let us note this briefly in three of his prayers for the enduement of believers with spiritual understanding and power.

Eph. 3:14-19: "For this cause I bow my knees unto the Father of our Lord Jesus Christ,

"Of whom the whole family in heaven and earth is named.

"That He would grant you, according to the riches of His glory, to be STRENGTHENED WITH MIGHT by His Spirit, in the inner man;

"That Christ may dwell in your hearts by faith; that ye, being rooted and grounded in love,

"May be ABLE TO COMPREHEND with all saints what is the breadth, and length, and depth, and height;

"And TO KNOW THE LOVE OF CHRIST, which passeth knowledge, THAT YE MIGHT BE FILLED WITH ALL THE FULNESS OF GOD."

Col. 1:9-11: "For this cause we also, since the day we heard it, do not cease to pray for you, and to desire THAT YE MIGHT BE FILLED WITH THE KNOWLEDGE OF HIS WILL IN ALL WISDOM AND SPIRITUAL UNDERSTANDING;

"That ye might walk worthy of the Lord unto all pleasing, being fruitful in every good work, and INCREASING IN THE KNOWLEDGE OF GOD;

"STRENGTHENED WITH ALL MIGHT, ACCORDING TO HIS GLORIOUS POWER, unto all patience and longsuffering with joyfulness."

This power, rather than the power to work miracles, is doubtless what Paul refers to in I Thes. 1:5:

"FOR OUR GOSPEL CAME NOT UNTO YOU IN WORD ONLY, BUT ALSO IN POWER, AND IN THE HOLY GHOST, AND IN MUCH ASSURANCE."

Further on in Colossians 1, where the apostle declares that God would have His saints know "what is the riches of the glory of this mystery among the Gentiles" (1:27), he continues:

Col. 1:28—2:3: "Whom we preach, WARNING EVERY MAN, AND TEACHING EVERY MAN IN ALL WISDOM; THAT WE MAY PRESENT EVERY MAN PERFECT IN CHRIST JESUS:

"Whereunto I also labor, striving according to His working, which worketh in me mightily.

"For I would that ye knew what great conflict I have for you, and for them at Laodicea, and for as many as have not seen my face in the flesh;

"That their hearts might be comforted, being knit together in love, and unto all riches of THE FULL ASSURANCE OF UN-DERSTANDING, to the acknowledgment [Gr., epignosis, "full knowledge"] of the mystery of God, and of the Father, and of Christ;

"In whom are hid all the treasures of wisdom and knowledge."

How different are these prayers from the prayers most frequently offered for babes in Christ! The apostle knew, and was inspired to write to the saints, that spiritual *power* comes from spiritual *understanding;* that only as we are "filled with *the knowledge of His will*" can we "walk *worthy* of the Lord unto all pleasing, being *fruitful* in every good work . . . *strengthened with all might, according to His glorious power*" (Col. 1:9-11).

The Church has dismally failed to grasp the significance of this great passage. It is constantly interpreted to mean that we should know God's will *for our lives.* Sincere young people are taught to ask God to show them: "Should I be a missionary in Africa, Asia, Europe? Or, should I be a pastor or Christian worker in a church at home? Or, perhaps, does He want me to go into business and help provide the needs for the Lord's work?"

This may all have its place, but *not* the *first* place, and it is *not* what the above passages refer to. We say with deep earnestness to those who have thus misunderstood its meaning: whether you go to Africa, Asia or Europe, or whether you remain at home as a pastor, Christian worker or businessman, will make little difference if you do not know "*HIS WILL*," i.e., *what He is doing and what He wants done in this dispensation of grace.* Acquire this knowledge, and you may be sure that He will graciously lead you as to His will for your life. To know "His will," you must pray for "all wisdom and spiritual understanding," so as to understand His Word to us. Thus alone will you be "strengthened with all might, by His Spirit, in the inner man." And to prayer must be added diligent Bible study, for this spiritual understanding is not granted by some miraculous demonstration in response to prayer alone. It is rather the result of prayerful, painstaking obedience to II Tim. 2:15:

"STUDY TO SHOW THYSELF APPROVED UNTO GOD, A WORKMAN THAT NEEDETH NOT TO BE ASHAMED, RIGHTLY DIVIDING THE WORD OF TRUTH."

As we sincerely obey this command we will come to enjoy one of the most precious blessings of the Christian life: "*the full assurance of understanding*"!

In Heb. 10:22 we read of "*the full assurance of faith.*" Precious possession!

In Heb. 6:11 the apostle writes of "*the full as-*

surance of hope."[1] This is even more blessed to experience.

But in Col. 2:2 we learn of the apostle's longing that the saints might enjoy *"the full assurance of understanding."* This is the most blessed of all, for by it we are enabled and emboldened to proclaim His Word in *"the power of the Spirit."*

How can we sincerely read these three prayers of the Apostle Paul without earnestly longing for this assurance and the boldness that goes with it, that we might indeed be *"fruitful in every good work"!*

---

1. "Which hope we have as an anchor to the soul, both sure and steadfast" (Ver. 19).

It Won't Be Easy

Chapter IX

FAITHFULNESS TO OUR COMMISSION

We have seen that in Paul's day his *"preaching of Jesus Christ according to the revelation of the mystery"* encountered opposition on every hand. For faithfully proclaiming this glorious message he was constantly called upon to bear affliction and reproach. In his last letter, written from prison in Rome, he calls attention to the distinctive character of his message, and adds:

"Wherein I suffer trouble as an evil doer, even unto bonds . . ." (II Tim. 2:7-9).

The almost constant suffering to which the apostle of grace was subjected naturally had its effect upon timid souls. Some, who saw the truth and the glory of his message, lacked the courage to stand with him in making it known. Others, who had started with him were tempted to—and some did—turn back.

In the light of all this it is not strange that Paul should write to Timothy:

"FOR GOD HATH NOT GIVEN US THE SPIRIT OF FEAR; BUT OF POWER, AND OF LOVE, AND OF A SOUND MIND.

"BE NOT THOU THEREFORE ASHAMED OF THE TESTIMONY OF OUR LORD, NOR OF ME HIS PRISONER: BUT BE THOU PARTAKER OF THE AFFLICTIONS OF THE

133

GOSPEL ACCORDING TO THE POWER OF GOD" (II Tim. 1:7,8).

Nor is it strange that the apostle should urge his son in the faith to *"be strong in the grace that is in Christ Jesus"* and to *"endure hardness as a good soldier of Jesus Christ,"* especially since *he himself* needed constant help in this regard.

Oh, that all who have come to see the glory of the gospel of the grace of God would pray for boldness to proclaim it, as Paul did in Eph. 6:19,20 and elsewhere!

Some may suppose that it would require little boldness *today* to proclaim grace in all its purity. Who is ever persecuted now, at least in free, enlightened lands, for preaching God's grace? Ah, but do not be deceived. Satan was no less active in his opposition to the truth when Constantine exalted the professing Church to prominence than when his predecessors persecuted the Church and sent its members to death by fire and sword. Indeed, the devil was doubtless *more successful* in Constantine's day than he had been when persecution raged. And does any believer in the Word of God suppose that Satan has relented in his opposition to the truth today just because men, at least in this land, are not burned at the stake or thrown to the lions? Do not be misled. Satan's enmity against God and against His Word continues undiminished. His hatred of "the gospel of the grace of God" is as bitter, and his opposition to it as determined as they ever were. But well does he know that the look of scorn is often more effective than the fiery sword. Well does he know that the

134

constant discouragements connected with being in the minority often succeed in silencing those who would stand courageously against physical persecution.

Let us, who know and love the truth, then, determine by God's grace that *nothing* shall make us unfaithful to our glorious commission; that, whatever the cost, we shall faithfully and boldly proclaim to others the unadulterated gospel of the grace of God, *"the preaching of Jesus Christ, according to the revelation of the mystery."*

A Closing Appeal

Chapter X

A WELL-ROUNDED MESSAGE

But must we always be preaching about the mystery revealed to Paul? Would not this be one-sided? Would it not be riding a hobby?

Well, was Ezra riding a hobby in proclaiming the law of Moses to Israel day after day? No, for this was God's program for his day. Were the twelve apostles riding a hobby as they went everywhere proclaiming "the gospel of the kingdom"? No, this was the message they had been *sent* to proclaim. The Pharisees and scribes were probably the ones who were giving equal time to all parts of the Jewish Bible, but had they been in the will of God they would have joined the apostles in accepting and proclaiming "the gospel of the kingdom," using the Old Testament Scriptures rather to confirm the God-given message.

Was Paul riding a hobby in his constant proclamation of grace? No, for this was the ministry which he had "received of the Lord Jesus" (Acts 20:24). In Eph. 3:2,3 he asks his readers "if ye have heard of *the dispensation of the grace of God which is given me to you-ward; how that by revelation He made known unto me the mystery.*" This was the message he was *commissioned* to proclaim, and he rightly called it "my gospel" (Rom. 16:25, *et al*). It is *our* gospel too, and we should never apologize for proclaiming it consistently.

Those who suppose that this means that we must keep harping on one string, as it were, only betray their ignorance of the broad scope of this great body of truth. We shall never fully measure the breadth and length and depth and height of it (Eph. 3:18,19), but as we keep measuring we come to experience more and more "the love of Christ, which passeth knowledge" (Eph. 3:19).[1] In II Cor. 4:7 God calls it a *"treasure."* In Col. 1:27 He says that He would have His saints know *"the riches of the glory"* of it. In II Tim. 1:14 He calls it a *"precious deposit,"* committed to our trust. When *God* uses such phraseology we may be sure that what He refers to was not purchased at a dime store! How could we possibly dispense all these riches of God in one sermon, or five, or ten, or ten thousand!

Those who fail to faithfully fulfil this great commission often talk of a "well-rounded ministry" and quote II Tim. 3:16 to support their position. The difficulty is, however, that they generally read into this passage what it does not say and they fail to read the *whole* statement to see what it *does* say.

II Tim. 3:16,17 does not say, nor does it imply, that we should give *equal time or emphasis* to all parts of the Word of God. It states rather that *"all Scripture is given by inspiration of God, and is profitable*

---

1. See the author's booklet, *The Dimensions of the Mystery, or Measuring the Immeasurable.*

for doctrine, for reproof, for correction, for instruction in righteousness, that THE MAN OF GOD may be perfect, THOROUGHLY FURNISHED unto all good works." Thus all Scripture is God-breathed and is profitable to us *in the proclamation of our God-given message*, especially since the mystery revealed to Paul casts light on all the Word of God and is confirmed by it. One has rightly called the mystery "the golden key that unlocks the Scriptures."

Is it not significant in this connection that Paul's declaration in II Tim. 3:16 is preceded by that in II Tim. 2:15:

"Study to show thyself approved unto God, a workman that needeth not to be ashamed, rightly dividing the Word of truth."

But does not II Tim. 4:2 say: *"Preach the Word"?* Yes, and some have taken this to mean that all parts of the Bible are to be given equal emphasis in our preaching. More mature reflection, however, should convince us that this is not so but that the apostle here calls *his* God-given message *"the Word."* If a man preaches obedience to the ceremonial law from Leviticus and Deuteronomy, is he preaching the Word? Certainly not in the sense that Paul intended it. If he exhorts his hearers from the Gospels and early Acts to sell all their possessions and have "all things common," is he preaching the Word? If he preaches from Mark 16:16 and Acts 2:38, and tells the lost: "Repent, and be baptized for the remission of sins," is he preaching the Word? Certainly not in the sense that the apostle meant it in II Tim. 4:2, for the Scriptures must be "rightly divided" and all

138

these passages must be considered in the light of the "mystery," the secret revealed through Paul.

A GRAVE RESPONSIBILITY

The same apostle who declares that all Scripture is inspired and profitable, also emphasizes our grave responsibility to guard faithfully and dispense wisely the blessed message committed to him and to us. See his exhortations to young Timothy:

I Tim. 6:3-5: "If any man teach otherwise, and consent not to wholesome words, even the words of our Lord Jesus Christ, and to the doctrine which is according to godliness, he is . . . destitute of the truth . . . from such withdraw thyself."

I Tim. 6:20: "O Timothy, keep that which is committed to thy trust. . . ."

II Tim. 1:13,14: "Hold fast the form of sound words which thou hast heard of me. . . . That good thing which was committed unto thee [Lit., "that precious deposit"] keep by the Holy Ghost which dwelleth in us."

II Tim. 2:2: "And the things that thou hast heard of me among many witnesses, the same commit thou to faithful men, who shall be able to teach others also."

II Tim. 2:7-9: "Consider what I say, and the Lord give thee understanding in all things.

"Remember that Jesus Christ, of the seed of David, was raised from the dead according to my gospel,

"Wherein I suffer trouble as an evil doer, even unto bonds; but the Word of God is not bound."

The times have changed, to be sure, but not our commission. The great revelation of grace first committed to Paul, and then to his associates, and then to other "faithful men," is our great commission still. It has never been superseded or annulled, and it has certainly not yet been fulfilled. If we fail to obey it, or if we neutralize or water it down to accommodate ourselves to the confusion of our times we are derelict in our duty and will answer to God for it.

CONCLUSION

Is not this the time to rededicate ourselves, or perhaps to dedicate ourselves for the first time, to the proclamation of this glorious message committed to us?

Eph. 1:9 declares that God *has "made known unto us the mystery of His will."* In Col. 1:9 the apostle prays that believers might be *"filled with the knowledge of His will,* in all wisdom and spiritual understanding,"* and in Chapter 4, Verse 12, he reminds the saints that others are praying that they might *"stand perfect and complete in all the will of God."*

We have no right to choose our own calling. God says: *"Ye are not your own: ye are bought with a price,"* and whatever the details involved, it is clear that it is *His* will that we spend our brief existence on earth making known to others the blessed message which He has commissioned us to proclaim. If you can *best* accomplish this by becoming a farmer or physicist, by teaching mathematics or going into business, this is fine, but none of us should ever forget— none has a right to forget—what it is that God has commissioned us, as His ambassadors, to do.

Each one of us must ask himself: "Why has God left me in this world? What is my responsibility to Him and to those about me?" It is good to stop every so often and ask ourselves such questions lest

140

our lives be frittered away to no purpose when God would make our service for Him vital and effective and would use us, each in his own way, to make some significant contribution to our generation.

What good if we learn everything under the sun, but do not even understand the mighty message He has committed to our trust? What will it profit us to become noted in any field, including the ministry, if we fail to fulfil God's purpose for us or to make known to others the blessed truths He has left us here to proclaim? It is fine to have a keen intellect, but God wants an intellect *and a heart* on fire to make His grace known to a dying world.

How the world and the Church need dedicated believers who will forget position or temporal gain and place themselves at God's disposal for *service;* who will gladly toil and suffer, trusting God alone to supply their needs, so that others may come to rejoice in the riches of His grace.

This is a high and holy calling, and not to be despised. Perhaps you have heard of the capable young pastor in a small country church, who was offered a lucrative position by a representative of a large business firm. When he declined the offer, the representative pressed him further, assuring him that the salary suggested could be raised considerably, perhaps even doubled, adding: "That would be many times what you are getting here." Finally the pastor said: "Let me explain it in this way. I have a big job here with a small salary. You are offering me a small job with a big salary. I prefer the former—the big job with the small salary." This pastor had things in clear perspective.

Paul suffered trouble, imprisonment and death as the bond-slave of Christ to make this blessed message known and we are still reaping the luscious fruit. Again and again the apostle says, by divine inspiration: *"Be ye followers of me."* Will you heed the call? Will you change your plans completely, if necessary, to offer yourself to God in unremitting service to make known to others those glorious truths we are commissioned to proclaim? If God's people will do this, our mission stations will not go unmanned; our Sunday Schools will not lack teachers; our small churches will not go without pastors. Rather these churches will gain inspired leaders and will become larger churches and great spiritual victories will be won for the Christ who loved us and died for us.

God bless our readers, each one, and use you, not merely in some secondary way, but to the fullest possible extent, to make known to others "the exceeding riches of His grace."

If this book has proved a blessing to you, why not help us get it out to others.

WRITINGS BY THE SAME AUTHOR

THINGS THAT DIFFER
The Fundamentals of Dispensationalism
Hardcover   279 Pages

MOSES AND PAUL
The Dispensers of Law and Grace
Hardcover   78 Pages

THE TWOFOLD PURPOSE OF GOD
Prophecy and Mystery
Hardcover   81 Pages

TWO MINUTES WITH THE BIBLE
A Daily Bible Study Devotional
Hardcover   366 Pages

TRUE SPIRITUALITY
The Secret of a Blessed Christian Experience
Hardcover   209 Pages

*Send for A Full Price List of Our Literature
and
Our Free Bible Study Monthly*
THE BEREAN SEARCHLIGHT

BEREAN BIBLE SOCIETY
PO Box 756
Germantown, WI 53022-0756
(Metro Milwaukee)

HELP US GET THE MESSAGE OUT

EXPLANATORY NOTE: Asterisks (*) indicate that the Scripture reference referred to is found more than one time on the given page.